THE
GHOST-HUNTING
CASEBOOK

NATALIE OSBORNE-THOMASON

D1456771

BLANDFORD

For Laurie, a special son who shares his mother's interest in the macabre and bizarre world that we live in.

A BLANDFORD BOOK

First published in the UK 1999
by Blandford
Cassell plc
Wellington House
125 Strand
London WC2R OBB

A Cassell imprint
Copyright © 1999 Natalie Osborne-Thomason
The right of Natalie Osborne-Thomason to be identified as the author of this
work has been asserted by her under the provisions of the UK Copyright,
Designs and Patents Act 1988.

Distributed in the United States by Sterling Publishing Co., Inc.,
387 Park Avenue South, New York, NY 10016–8810

A Cataloguing-in-Publication Data entry for this title is available and may
be obtained from the British Library

ISBN 0-7137-2768-3

Designed by Chris Bell
Printed in Great Britain by MPG Books Ltd, Bodmin, Cornwall

CONTENTS

STONE TAPE RECORDINGS 45

SNIPPETS OF THE PAST 67

HARMLESS HAUNTINGS 85

ACKNOWLEDGEMENTS

VERY SPECIAL THANKS are due to the following for their invaluable help while I was compiling this book: the writer and scientist Albert Budden, who had many good ideas and constructive criticisms; Patrick Leonard, for the magnificent photography and help in compiling and researching some of the cases; Linda Thomason, Kate Snowling and my mum; Gary Stock for all of his stories, letters and phone calls, and generous time. Thanks also to all of the numerous kind people from all over Britain who bothered to write to me telling me of their experiences. It takes time and effort to write a letter, which sadly today is a dying art. Laurie Lee boosted my confidence when I was at a particularly low ebb and inspired me to put pen to paper as a child after reading *Cider with Rosie*. I should also like to thank the various publicans who allowed me to write about the 'spirits' in their hostelries, and not forgetting two fellow Ghost Club Society members, Robert Snow and Dennis Moyses. Thanks go finally to Gemma, Laurie and Becky, my children, for being so patient when I spent hours away or at the typewriter and ignored them, when all I wanted to do was write up my case notes.

Thank you all!

INTRODUCTION

THE REASONS for writing this book are many and varied. Firstly, having completed my first book, *Walking Through Walls*, I quickly realized that I had much more to write on the subject. It was as if I had just brushed lightly at the surface; I still had much more to find out. I needed to delve deeper into the many mysterious occurrences that are grouped together and labelled 'hauntings'.

Once people find out that you are a ghost investigator, the letters and contacts just keep pouring in, especially after a radio broadcast or newspaper article which I am occasionally asked to do. This is not surprising, however, as the phenomenon is all too common. I still had a dozen cases left over from my first book, and new ones coming in all the time. I had also come to some important new conclusions, partly due to a scientific breakthrough from Canada.

It is hard to remember when I first became interested in this subject. It could well have been during the many childhood holidays that our family spent touring Scotland, staying in beautiful old remote farmhouses with views of mountains and heather – even the odd castle or two. It did seem then that nearly every old building we stayed in overnight had its own ghosts.

I particularly remember one night spent in a very old Scottish house. My sister and I were sleeping in a big, antique, dusty, tapestry-curtained four-poster bed. My dad had teased me before bedtime about the apparition that always walked the landing corridors at night. I was desperate to go to the toilet in the middle of the night, but when I peeped my head around the bedroom door into the quiet corridor I saw to my horror a figure clad in full armour standing next to the toilet door. In the half-dark, I was sure that he moved; so, scared and trembling, I leapt back into the safety of my bed, drawing all the curtains around me for protection. In the morning, the suit of armour – for that's what the 'ghost' was – had lost his menace, and I ran to the toilet relieved. All my silly childish fears had gone with the welcome coming of the daylight.

I'm sure that some of the places we stopped in did have their own genuine ghosts. Since those early days of devouring any books I could on the subject of ghosts and monsters, and as a teenager staying up late every Saturday night to watch the seemingly endless stream of 'Hammer House of Horror' films, I have always believed that this world does have its own population of ghosts, and even the odd monster (well, maybe in Loch Ness).

After growing up, getting married, and having three children, for the first time I encountered one of these ghosts in my own house. The experience surprised even me and I was scared. Yet, if you have to live in a house that is haunted, you just have to accept it, or move out. It's easier by far to accept it. In the end, any odd occurrences are hardly noticed any more than an annoying dripping tap or creaking floorboards. You just take it as being part and parcel of the very fabric of the house.

For the past four years, since becoming a member of the Ghost Club Society and a paranormal investigator, my belief in the strange world that sometimes infringes upon our own remains unshaken. There is a pattern and symmetry to the phenomenon of ghosts. Whether it be a poltergeist outbreak in a modern family home or a so-called 'anniversary ghost' seen only once a year, these patterns are there for all to see. You just have to know where to look.

I hope as you delve into the many cases outlined in this book you will see the patterns too. Maybe, however, we will never understand or prove the existence of this phenomenon. For, as the sceptics rightly say, photographs can be faked, people can lie and the human imagination is a wonderful thing. It is good to have a healthy scepticism, but when you have seen and felt invisible hands around your neck or seen objects move by themselves in front of your eyes apparently of their own volition, as I have, you cannot help but be sure. The world is at times a very strange place indeed.

So, in the pages that follow, the mystery will unfold and slowly reveal its many colours. Some answers have appeared on rare occasions, and these I shall share. A subject of such universal appeal is simply a treat to investigate and write about. I hope that my enthusiasm for my chosen field translates onto the written page, and that this book is as enjoyable to read as it was to compile. Happy ghost-hunting.

NOTE

Some of the people who have recounted their experiences to me requested to remain anonymous. In such instances I have either changed their name completely or only used the first letter of their surname. Others were quite happy for me to use full names and place names in the text. Unless otherwise stated, places mentioned in this book are located in the UK.

MALEVOLENT HAUNTINGS

FORTUNATELY, this is by far the smallest category of hauntings, comprising perhaps only about 10 per cent of cases, but malevolent hauntings do occur. The following stories show that harm can be done through this type of ghostly activity, be it from stress-induced illness that is a direct result of the experiences, or from the so-called spiritual possession, real or imagined, of the unfortunate victim. If we suppose, for the sake of argument, that some ghosts are the restless souls of the dead interacting with our environment, then we must expect that, just as there are good and bad people in the world, there must be both benign and harmful ghosts.

People who have experienced a malevolent haunting have often likened it to having an intruder in their home – an intruder that cannot be seen or captured, which just makes the situation much worse for the family or person besieged. In my experience, such homes and buildings are difficult or even impossible to sell. The very atmosphere of the place puts off potential purchasers. So, if the family try to flee from the situation, escape is made difficult.

The rooms affected will often take on an unnatural chill, despite central heating or fires. In one case I looked at, even the light in the room seemed to have been affected. Despite a very large bay window, it was dark all year round, all through the day, and full of shadows. Such an atmosphere is obviously not conducive to the happiness of anyone concerned. Added to this, there can be the disruption of noises in the night, or objects being moved around and even destroyed by fires or flooding, the cause of which is not easily determined.

A good example of this was the famous Enfield poltergeist case (see Case 97) in the mid-1970s, when a family of five were held in torment for many months. The situation quickly developed into a media circus. The family were helped, though, by the timely intervention of the Society for Psychical Research (SPR) and investigator Maurice Grosse. Thankfully, their ordeal eventually ended and the family could at last pick up the pieces and start again with their lives.

The answers to this type of haunting are often as elusive to everyone concerned as the malicious ghost. Careful investigation and a pinch of scepticism are the order of the day when encountering these scenarios. If the family holds any religious convictions, having an exorcism or blessing performed can be helpful. Checking into the background and history of the building is always useful too.

Any dreadful event that happened in a building – for example, a murder or sudden death, continued bitter feuding between people, or fear and deep unhappiness – can leave behind a sort of psychic imprint. It is as if the very bricks and stones can soak up the raw emotions involved, allowing them to leak back out at a later date. On the pages that follow are just a few examples of such cases; we can all be extremely relieved, perhaps, that they didn't happen to us.

CASE 1 — THE DEMON IN THE PICTURE

THE FOLLOWING story was told to me by Tarona Hawkins from Leicester. Even though it happened some time ago, it still makes her shiver to recall the tale. The experience was the most frightening of her life.

Tarona was visiting her friend Maxine in another district on a rare evening off from work. The two were talking when they heard an unexpected knock at the window. It was Maxine's sister, whom Tarona had not seen since her wedding some years before. She tried to conceal her shock when the girl entered the house, as this once-beautiful woman now looked a worn-out wreck.

They all sat drinking coffee and Maxine's sister told them that she had split up with her husband. All had been well with the marriage until her husband received a promotion. He became manager of a large super-market following the death of the previous manager. It had taken him a year to build up the store, and in that time he had become a different person. At first, his wife thought he was having an affair; he became violent and constantly complained of bad headaches. He went for a brain scan, but no sign of disease or abnormality was found.

The last straw came when the husband refused to go to a family wedding. Maxine's sister went alone, making excuses for her husband's absence. However, he turned up at the reception unexpectedly, and appeared to be something of his old self, even asking his wife to dance. A guest started to take photographs, and took one of the pair dancing. Suddenly the husband went berserk, for no apparent reason, and started a vicious attack on the person who had taken the snapshot. After a very embarrassing scene, the couple were told to leave.

When they got home, he beat up his wife so badly that she had to stay in hospital for two weeks. It was agreed that she would not prosecute if he would move out of the marital home. When she finally came out of hospital and arrived home, he had taken everything from the house, not even leaving his wife a bed to sleep in.

Tarona asked Maxine's sister what on earth had made her husband so angry at having his photograph taken, at which point Maxine went to a drawer and brought out a selection of photo albums. It was in one of these photos that Tarona saw 'it', directly above his shoulder. The only thing she could liken it to was a 'gremlin' creature, just like those in the well-known series of films.

Tarona asked the two sisters if the whole incident could have been a trick; that is, had anyone taken a gremlin-like toy to the reception, or was anyone in fancy dress that day. The answer was an emphatic 'no'; soon afterwards Maxine's sister left, and Tarona told Maxine her views on the photograph.

Being a psychic, Tarona has always had the ability to 'read' people from photographs, and she tells me that she had never seen anything like the creature in the photograph. Gently, she pointed out the spot in the photo and told Maxine that she believed it to be some kind of demonic spirit. Alarmed, Maxine took all the photos of the wedding in question and burned them, begging Tarona not to tell her sister her views on the photo as her problems over the past year had been horrendous. Roughly a year later, Tarona received a telephone call from Maxine, saying her ex-brother-in-law had died from cancer.

This case would seem to have all the hallmarks of a demonic

possession; or perhaps the man's illness had started well before it was medically diagnosed and it somehow affected his personality to a devastating degree.

The Japanese believe that the unfortunate can sometimes become targets for evil spirits. These spirits are said to attach themselves to the back of the victim and are notoriously difficult to remove. Most cultures do not subscribe to the view of evil spirits able to possess the weak, but the Catholic church usually has an exorcist working in each diocese. I can remember meeting one of these, and was impressed by his calm demeanour and imposing presence.

All the people that I have met over the past four years since beginning my research in this field seem unable to forget their brushes with malevolent ghosts. They make a deep impression on the witness, and often the researcher too.

CASE 2 THE EXORCIST

GARY STOCK is a medium exorcist who works in the Bermondsey area of London. The very nature of his job brings him into contact with all sorts of unusual hauntings of both buildings and people. The case that follows was related to me by Gary himself, and it concerns an 11-year-old girl called Sascha. It is just one of the 40 or more exorcisms that he has conducted, and fortunately the end result was satisfactory.

At the beginning of the summer of 1996 the little girl had become withdrawn and depressed. She would not mix with other children and told her parents that she was being tormented by a spirit that seemed to want to possess her. Sometimes she would hear voices in her head and she became distant from her parents. All this behaviour was at odds with the little girl Sascha had been before.

Puzzled and distressed, and unable to understand their child's behaviour, Sascha's parents contacted Gary. They had heard of his work and thought maybe he could help. Conventional wisdom would have diagnosed a possible mental disorder in Sascha, so perhaps the couple felt they had nothing to lose in taking advice from the very unconventional Mr Stock.

It was a Monday evening when Gary visited Sascha and asked her what was troubling her. He then told her to sit down, and laid his hands on her head, telling her to try to envisage a bright, strong, white light. The spirit was then commanded to leave and a powerful force was felt to be ejected from the child. Since then, the girl has returned to her cheerful, sociable self, and has also become close to her parents once more.

Following this case, Gary's work with people experiencing hauntings of all kinds has continued, and he has been asked to appear on Sky TV live to talk about his cases. Word of Gary's exciting work has got as far as Germany, and he was recently sent to Yorkshire with a German television crew to film one of his exorcisms. He is able to work by envisaging a powerful light when asking the spirit to depart. He also commonly uses holy water, with which he sprinkles the possessed and the afflicted building to cleanse them of evil. Often, after one of these ceremonies, for a while his own health suffers.

Such after-effects can last for hours or days following the exorcism. However, this hasn't in any way put Gary off his work. He feels it to be something that only few are called to do, and if led towards it one cannot easily turn away.

CASE 3 THE PILLOW

IN THE early 1990s, in the small village of Bishopsbourne in Kent, Andy Capon had a nocturnal encounter that terrified him so much he will never forget it. He experienced the vivid re-enactment of a crime that took place in a previous century. The mark of that dreadful event had remained even though the two principal players had long since died.

Andy was seeing a girl called Harriet at the time and she and her parents lived in an eighteenth-century cottage in Bishopsbourne. Harriet's parents were on holiday, and the couple were looking after the cottage for two weeks. It was a Saturday evening, and Harriet had invited a few friends round for drinks and a chat. Andy became tired, and at about midnight he excused himself and went off to bed (he stressed to me that he was sober at the time). He lay in bed for about ten minutes, and was in that pleasant state in between consciousness and sleep when he felt a pressure bearing down on him and smothering him. As Andy struggled for breath and snapped back into consciousness, he realized with horror that the pressure on his body and the smothering on his face were getting stronger.

He remembers struggling to push upwards and remove the force, which felt like a very strong man sitting astride him and holding a pillow over his face. This went on for some seconds, until Andy heard Harriet coming upstairs. Despite this, the pressure continued until Harriet actually entered the room, whereupon her boyfriend finally managed to break free and leap out of bed screaming and perspiring.

Naturally, Harriet was upset to see him in this state, and Andy told her shakily what had happened. She put it down to a bad dream. The couple went to bed and Andy eventually went to sleep, thankfully without any further interruptions.

At breakfast the next morning, Harriet told Andy the reason for his experience the previous night. She could not tell him at the time as it would have frightened him more and she did not want Andy to leave her alone in her parents' 'haunted' house. Apparently, the main bedroom in the cottage had been haunted for many years, because in the eighteenth century one of the previous owners of the timber-framed house had murdered his wife by smothering her with a pillow until she suffocated. It would seem that the murderer's spirit, not that of his victim, haunts the house. This was Andy's first brush with a ghost, and he hopes it will be his last.

What I find astonishing about this case is that Andy claims to have known nothing of the murder, and so it is hard to put it down to the coincidence of a vivid dream. It is also unlikely to have been a type of sleep paralysis (when a person wakes up and experiences a few seconds during which they are unable to move a muscle), which the brain naturally causes to stop us physically acting out our dreams.

CASE 4 — THE CAT

THE NEXT story, related to me by Colin P of Derby, happened during the winter of 1978. At the time of the incident Colin was sharing a house in Erdington in the north-east of Birmingham. He was a member of a local amateur dramatic society, which had a theatre that was about a 15-minute walk from his house.

At the end of the street in which the theatre was situated was a winebar, popular with the actors after rehearsals. It was late one night in November and some of the actors had been for a couple of pints. Colin walked from the theatre with his friend Martin, who lived close by. After saying goodnight to his friend, Colin continued the walk home on his own as usual. The road curved up ahead, and to the left was a local railway station, Wylde Green, near Erdington. It was a shortcut to pass by along the platform of the station, and indeed he had done so many times without any trepidation, in all weathers.

On this cold, misty night, as he mounted the ramp of the platform, Colin felt very uneasy for no apparent reason. Even when recounting the tale to me nearly 20 years later, he felt cold and shivery at the thought. Suddenly he noticed a brilliant white cat walking towards him along the platform. Oddly, he felt that the cat was not an ordinary one; furthermore, it took absolutely no notice of Colin. As it had been his experience that cats tend to be timid, and watch people very closely as they approach, this in itself seemed odd. The cat slowly approached him and Colin had to step out of its path. He told me that he has never experienced the like of it before or since. He felt certain that the cat was not of this world, because of the atmosphere in the station that night and also the very actions of the ghostly animal. After the two had passed, the frightened actor did not dare look back and the feeling of dread did not leave him until he had cleared the vicinity of the station, by the other ramp at the end of the platform.

Intrigued by it all, the next day he went back in the daylight, but the atmosphere of malevolence had completely disappeared. Nearby an old lady kept cats, so the next time Colin saw her he asked her if she owned a white one; she said no, only a black-and-white one. She also knew of no white cats locally.

Colin stressed to me that he was not drunk at the time the incident took place. Also, he felt uneasy before he even saw the cat: 'It was as if the whole station was held in the grip of the animal's awful presence.' Needless to say, for a couple of weeks Colin avoided the station after the hours of darkness.

5 EXORCISM

CAROL, TERRY and their three small children found their 1920s town-centre house in Northampton to be haunted by not one but two distinct ghosts. Lights turned on and off by themselves and the baby was often found wrapped tightly in his cot blankets (in a way that his mother never left him). A dark-cloaked figure was also seen going up and down the stairs.

After I visited them on a number of occasions and interviewed them at some length, they telephoned me to tell me that the haunting had taken a frightening turn. The two oldest children, both aged under five, shared a bedroom. One evening Carol went to check on them before going to bed herself, but found she could not open the door. As there was no lock on the door, she was puzzled, but thought the children must have put something in front of the door which prevented it from being opened. She called out to them, and Terry came and pushed heavily against the door. Suddenly it opened. The two children were both fast asleep and there was nothing behind the door that could have blocked it.

Carol was very frightened, because she knew the door had not stuck – it was very loose-fitting. She told me it felt as if a heavy person was learning against it, preventing her from getting to her children.

When this happened again, this time when the children were both awake and very upset, she asked me if I would bring along to the house a friend of mine, Reverend Bill Simons, to exorcize the ghosts. The vicar came and performed the exorcism, which consisted of a series of prayers said in each room of the house. The last room that he entered was the lounge, a scene of quite a lot of ghostly activity that had been witnessed by many, including a neighbour and some of the couple's relatives.

One girl felt and saw a dark, shadowy form sweep over her one afternoon as she sat on the sofa watching a video with Carol and the children. She leapt up, and bruised her leg on the coffee table. Such was her fright that she left the house and stood in the street, too scared to go back in, for quite some time. She had heard about the ghost, but had been sceptical.

As we all stood in the lounge, heads bent praying and asking the ghost to vacate the premises, I saw from the corner of my eye near the window a greyish, fuzzy-edged shadow that I had not noticed before.

When the prayers had finished and I spoke to the others about it, the mysterious shadow had gone.

I must admit that I had not believed the exorcism would work, but when I left the atmosphere there did seem to have improved. Usually when I visit a place that is haunted I am struck by an overwhelming feeling of depression, and I had felt this on the occasions I visited the home of Carol and Terry. However, this atmosphere seemed to have lifted, and I was very interested to find out, when I phoned the couple some weeks later, if anything had changed.

Indeed it had, and Carol was very pleased. There had been no more sightings of the man on the stairs and the lounge was warm for the first time (it had always been very chilly before). Unfortunately, this did not last. The family contacted me about 18 months after the exorcism and told me that a few strange things were happening again – footsteps, cold spots, etc. However, thankfully, the haunting never resumed its previous intensity. The young family then moved out so as to be nearer their elder daughter's new school. They didn't have too much difficulty selling the house, which surprised me.

CASE 6 — A BABY'S CRY

THIS EVENT took place in the early 1980s, but Eric Baldwin never forgot the incident which was also witnessed by five other people. Eric hails from Yorkshire, and he and a friend called Rita and her two-month-old baby were invited to stay at the old farmhouse home of a former schoolfriend. The farmhouse was situated on the Yorkshire moors; it was one of three houses joined together, and they were very isolated in position. Inside, the original oak beams crossed the ceilings, blackened by centuries of the soot from open fires.

During one of their evenings at the farmhouse, the two were invited next door to a birthday party. As the baby was fast asleep in its pram, they accepted the invitation. After about 20 minutes, Eric heard the baby screaming, and several of the party-goers went next door to find the baby still in its pram with a look of obvious alarm on its face. Rita ran over and picked up the baby to comfort it.

As soon as she did this, a strange thing happened: a large ham that had been hanging above the baby's pram dropped straight into the pram where the baby had been lying. (Hanging hams up to cure on 'S'-shaped butcher's hooks suspended from a beam in cool sculleries was commonly practised years ago by country folk.) Eric told me that if the ham, weighing several pounds, had fallen on the baby it could have caused serious injury. They had been foolish to place the pram beneath it, but Eric was puzzled by three things.

1   The ham was hanging on a heavy and strong butcher's hook suspended from the ceiling beam, and the hook was still intact; in fact, the ham was placed back safely on it afterwards.

2   Some unseen force must have lifted the ham before it could have dropped in front of the five witnesses.

3   Did the two-month-old baby somehow get a premonition that the object would drop into its pram, which woke it up, or was it a lucky coincidence?

Eric found the incident interesting, believing that the baby somehow knew of its possible fate and cried for its mother's help. Also, whatever force or agency detached the ham from the hook obviously had malevolent intent. Was it a ghost that haunted the cottage and took exception to the holidaymakers stopping there, particularly the baby? All concerned are very thankful and relieved that no-one was hurt. It could so easily have been a different story.

I have had a similar experience to this myself. It was in 1984, when we had just moved into an old cottage and I was expecting a baby. The building was on three floors and had only two bedrooms. My husband and I had the first-floor room and we intended to use the large attic room for our baby. However, before she was born I sometimes heard noises coming from this room, like furniture being moved about. It was always very cold and had a dreadful atmosphere. One day when I was alone in the house, I heard a banging on the walls upstairs. I gingerly went to investigate, and to my shock saw the light-pull cord seemingly being yanked by an invisible hand and continually smashing against the wall. I knew whatever it was to be evil, and I was scared. I ran downstairs and fetched a pair of scissors, with which I cut off the toggle on the light-pull, so that it couldn't make the noise. I had in fact heard the noise before, on occasion, and wondered what it was. I shouted at the thing to leave my house.

When the baby was a year old, and getting too big to share our room, instead of putting her in the near-empty attic room I made up her cot on the upstairs landing, keeping the affected bedroom door firmly shut. I had a strong feeling that if I put the baby in that room the evil (ghost, entity) might try to harm her. I knew somehow that it couldn't go further than the closed door.

We lived in that cottage for about three years and I never went in that attic room more than two or three times. Others didn't understand my strong feelings, but I didn't care. I had a feeling of evil in that place and my mother's instinct said 'no' to putting my baby in there.

CASE 7 | ME AND MY SHADOW

THE LARGE factory in Countess Road, St James, Northampton, is at least 100 years old and has had many different uses since it was built. In the early part of the 1980s, the building was divided up into two units, the left-hand side becoming a series of smart offices. During this period it was rented by a company, called Audio Visual Facilities, that specialized in conference work, film shows and hiring out video-type equipment of all descriptions, both local and nationwide.

My father had originally set up this company when I was in my early teens, and initially it was quite successful. I got an after-school job there as a cleaner, and had about three offices, a couple of storerooms and the toilets to clean each Saturday morning. Despite the place having been thoroughly modernized inside, some parts of it were decidedly creepy, especially the stairs. It was not only me who felt this while working at Countess Road for AVF; there were about five others, with various job descriptions, who had similar feelings.

During most of the time that my father and his business partner Martin leased the large building, the other half of it stood empty. One evening my father visited the offices late to drop off some equipment. He let himself in at the double outer doors and climbed the two wide flights of burgundy-carpeted stairs. He noticed his shadow as he unlocked the inner half-glazed door, but thought nothing of it, that is until he continued along the long corridor. The dark shadow then overtook his stride, and realization struck that it was *not* his shadow. It looked nothing like him; it was a different shape. It continued along to the end of the corridor, and then simply glided through the wall (this wall was a dead-end, built when the factory was divided).

My father was never one to be scared or bothered by such a thing, so he just put his equipment in the storeroom and locked up. He would probably never have mentioned it, except for the fact that many other weird things happened there. Often doors would open and close all by themselves. They were heavy firedoors, and so this should not have been possible. A woman working there joked that she had seen a little old lady busy opening and shutting these doors.

I believe that in some small way the old building was jinxed, as my father and his business had nothing but difficulties during his time there. There was a series of burglaries. The first time the burglars broke in at the front door, so it was reinforced. The next time they came in from next door, gaining entry through the roof by removing some polystyrene ceiling tiles. They were obviously disturbed in their endeavours, as they left some very valuable aluminium ladders. My father was pleased, as he needed some of these and they proved useful. The third and last attempt amazed even the police who investigated the robberies. The burglars came through from next door and, using a small explosive device, blew a large hole through the brick wall. However, they escaped with only a few mini-video machines.

Eventually my father and his partner fell out. My father left to continue business on his own again. Just before this, I contracted carbon-monoxide poisoning from the faulty boiler in a downstairs room. I spent some time near it one day, breathing in the fumes unknowingly during cleaning. Afterwards I slept and slept, feeling that I had a bad dose of the 'flu, or had been poisoned. After a few days I got over it. Most of the others working in the building had for days suffered from bad headaches, nausea and depression, until the faulty boiler was found and put right. The situation could have been much worse. It was not in my view a good place, and could well have been haunted.

Of course, it could all be a chain of coincidence with an hallucination or two thrown in for good measure. I don't believe this to be the case, as more than one person saw the ghost and its effects. Also, the negative energy seemingly operating in the offices is a common side-effect of malevolent hauntings. Hence, any building affected by a haunting of this type will often change hands rapidly, or be so difficult to sell owing to the bad atmosphere inside that it will remain empty for long periods. One case I covered in the early days concerned a similarly affected house. It had remained empty for years apparently without logical explanation, despite the property boom of the 1980s in Britain.

CASE 8 THE OLD HAG

MR WINSTON-SPARROW, an elderly artist living and working in Cornwall, wrote to me about his experiences in his house and attached artist's studio. These experiences were both unnerving and difficult to explain.

The artist has lived in his present home for the last 30 years; it was built in 1934. He believes his house to have been built on the demolished remains of an old cottage. There is a well in the garden that could have belonged to this earlier dwelling. In about 1994, Mr Winston-Sparrow was woken at 3am by a loud noise he described as sounding like a heavy coal hammer being dropped onto a wooden floor. To investigate the noise and attempt to discover where it had come from, he got out of bed and switched on the light. All at once he felt an intense presence of evil in the room.

This came as a shock, as having lived in his home for so many years he had never felt anything like it before. The evil presence felt so strong that he began to shiver from head to toe. He had no control over this; it was completely involuntary. Looking for the obvious, he went into his studio to see if a picture had fallen from its hook, causing him to wake. None of them had, and searching the house he could find nothing to account for the loud thud. He had little sleep that night and when he woke in the morning he was still very cold and shivering.

Since this incident two other odd things have repeatedly occurred in Mr Winston-Sparrow's home. He has heard a horrible croaking sound, and felt hands clawing at him. When this has happened, the same sense of evil has accompanied the phenomenon. He believes the 'ghost' to be that of a malevolent old woman.

The ghost in this story sounds remarkably like the legend of the 'old hag' – a term coined for the ghost of an old woman with evil intent. She is represented by the season of winter. There is a tradition of burying a stone at the end of winter which is known as 'burying the old hag of winter'. In doing this, we are supposed to be ridding ourselves symbolically of all the bad and upset in our lives, in the hope of finding happiness in the spring. Later, flowers are planted in the same spot. This is described in Cassandra Eason's book *Ghost Encounters*, together with other traditions associated with hauntings.

CASE 9 MY NAME IS RAGESH

HEATHER C and her daughter live in the Weston Favell area of Northampton. She contacted me because of her worries about the odd happenings taking place in her home. Heather lives in an extremely ordinary-looking 1970s house, which is owned by the local housing association.

I visited Heather and her daughter Jodi one evening in June 1998. During our long chat on the phone, Heather had told me that throughout a long period of poltergeist activity she had let into her home an assortment of psychics, mediums and clergy, in a vain attempt to find the cause of and a cure for the disturbances. Unfortunately, this had just brought with it even more confusion.

A psychic called André told her that it was all caused by a young Indian boy named Ragesh. He assured Mrs C that the spirit would accompany him home. It didn't, and the activity continued unabated.

Next came a local clergyman, Reverend Knight. He pronounced the house evil and pranced around, liberally sprinkling holy water as he went. Upstairs he found several of Heather's books on astrology and the occult, and he told her to get rid of them, believing, it would seem, that they could be behind the disturbances. Unsurprisingly, after the vicar departed Heather was once again left feeling upset and disappointed.

This pattern was to be repeated as Heather desperately tried to find some answers. She contacted a medium in Holland, who attempted to be of help but at that distance had little success.

When I visited the family, both mother and daughter quite understandably had little hope that I could answer any of their questions. I took a quick look around the house which is filled with paintings, lush green plants and various interesting foreign *objets d'art*. A less evil house one would be hard pressed to find. It is true that the area in which the house is situated is a little 'rough', but that's about all one could say. I went downstairs and spoke at length to Heather about the 'haunting'. A very strange story began to unravel itself. Like a tangled ball of wool, it was hard to find the real beginning, and I suspect that because of the psychology of the two people involved there may never be a satisfactory resolution.

Heather C said it all began about four or five years earlier. She lives on her own with her teenage daughter and has a son who is now in Scotland. She had separated from her husband some years before. She confided in me that she had suspected her daughter might have caused some of the phenomena, but certainly not all. The girl had been sexually abused at the age of seven by her grandfather. This had understandably left her very angry and upset. The mother wondered if this anger might have caused Jodi, at times, to cause the poltergeist-type activity, or perhaps copy it.

The list of examples of this activity is quite astonishing. It had caused much disruption to the two living in the house, and had gradually worn Heather down over the years. It started with messages stuck to the walls around the house, which they would find when they got up in the morning and went downstairs for breakfast. These messages were written in a childlike scrawl, and appeared to be from a boy called Ragesh. They were all fairly innocent in content; some were even quite amusing and clever. For example: 'My name is Ragesh. I am six. My mother was a jeweller.' Or: 'I think Jodi should go out with the boy at school and not the painter.' (At the time, their house was being painted by a very good-looking young man from the housing association and Jodi had confided to her mother that she fancied him.)

Also at this time little shopping lists would be found in the kitchen in the same handwriting, asking for cakes and sweets. These were usually on tiny scraps of paper.

There were various apports (mysteriously appearing objects) too: some tiny white mittens and bootees, a child's doll, collages and drawings. One afternoon Heather opened the freezer and was shocked to find a wooden face mask placed near the icecream. This had been a present from her son and was kept on the living-room wall. On another occasion, they came home to find the kitchen walls liberally 'painted' with sticky icing sugar. A whole box had been used, and Heather was cross as it took ages to scrub it all off.

When mother and daughter returned home once from a shopping trip, Jodi was frightened to discover a figure sitting on her bed. It was a cleverly constructed effigy made from some stuffed pyjamas, gloves and a pair of trainers, and looked quite lifelike. Heather took a photograph of it, as she sometimes did of the other bizarre phenomena.

She handed me a photograph, which showed a miscellaneous assortment of items of grocery shopping on the kitchen worktop. She had briefly turned around to put something away in a cupboard, and when she turned back, to her great surprise, on top of each item of shopping was a seedless grape balanced carefully on its end. Heather reported that she would often find their clothes soaking in the bath – clothes that had previously been hanging in the wardrobe. This naturally proved to be very annoying.

Many of the letters, photographs and apports were burned after Reverend Knight's visit, as he had told them that it was all very evil, and that by keeping these objects they would 'hold' the evil in their home. However, Heather has kept the dainty hand-knitted bootees and mittens, two of the letters and a few photographs.

After talking to the mother, at some length, and to her daughter, I concluded that some of the activity could well have been caused by her daughter, or even by herself either consciously or subconsciously. Obviously the evidence produced was all purely anecdotal, as indeed so much evidence and testimony often is. I saw nothing strange during my visit, although I didn't expect to. However, there was a peculiarly oppressive and heavy atmosphere on the landing, a feeling I have encountered in other haunted locations during my years of investigating.

I couldn't help but feel that all of the very natural anger and frustration caused by the sexual abuse was possibly behind some of the milder aspects and activity, and could be put down to telekinesis. I also felt the mother to be a highly psychic and intuitive person, who appeared to be a frustrated medium. I strongly suggested that she try to develop these skills instead of worrying to much about the haunting. It was best for them to forget the doom-laden spoutings of the vicar and some of the psychics. The house was not evil. Evil, of course, had been committed against the girl Jodi, and in turn had partly been involved in the phenomena they experienced.

When I left, I decided to retain an open mind about this case as some of the activity could indeed have been caused by a ghost, but most certainly not all of it. I promised to visit them again if they wanted me to and hoped that things would gradually calm down. I sincerely wish them well.

It is a sad fact that poltergeist-type hauntings tend to occur in homes where abuse or deep unhappiness are prevalent. This has quite naturally led some sceptics to conclude that it can all be put down to attention-seeking behaviour on the part of one or more of the occupants. While this may of course be the case in some instances, it is not true of them all. It is very often a combination of behavioural disturbance and ghostly disturbance.

PSYCHICS, SENSITIVES AND MEDIUMS

THIS CHAPTER is devoted to people who could be described as psychics, sensitives or mediums. These are the people who are more likely to see or hear ghosts. Often much against their wishes, they seem to possess faculties of awareness which many of us have lost – qualities that animals also appear to possess.

During many episodes of haunting it is often the family pet, be it cat or dog, who is first unsettled by and indeed notices the resident ghost. The animal might bark or hiss suddenly for no apparent reason, in the same spot in a room, often seemingly looking into thin air as no-one else in the room is able to see anything.

Psychic people seem to be able to use powers that I believe we all possess, but don't know how to tune into. Such gifted people have often remarked that they can feel the presence of a spirit or ghost through a sudden drop in the ambient room temperature. Their skin sometimes comes out in goosebumps, and quite often the atmosphere in the room becomes melancholy. It is as if, for the effects of ghostly activity to manifest, the agent needs a source of readily available energy. I think that this source could simply be heat.

The change in atmosphere in the room, which in my experience tends towards a depression of the feelings and emotions of those present, could be due to an increased electrical activity in the room which probably suppresses some of the normal brain function.

These are all just theories, of course, and perhaps we shall never uncover all of the answers. I feel, though, that it is beyond doubt, even in scientific circles, that people can and do use hidden powers in the brain, and these can be very strong. When we understand this process much more fully, we will at last begin to unravel the mysteries outlined in this book.

CASE 10 | PSYCHIC STUART

STUART SMITH, who comes from Wolverhampton, has had quite a few brushes with the unusual, including ghosts, in his lifetime and describes himself as 'quite psychic'. His most interesting experience happened when he was 14 years old and is possibly of the stone tape recording type.

On a winter's night, Stuart and a friend had wandered a little way outside their village, and decided to turn back. After passing through a small housing estate, the pair came near to a bridge that crosses a disused railway line. They stood for a moment talking. Stuart was looking down the road, on either side of which were tall bushes that created a dark passageway.

The boys continued walking when a big, black shadow moved slowly across their path, about 20 m (65 ft) in front of them. It appeared to be the shadow of a horse and rider. The rider looked hunched over with one arm hanging down and the other hand holding the reins. He was wearing a cloak with the hood pulled up over his head.

At first Stuart, slightly unnerved, said nothing to his friend, but when they got further along the road he asked his friend if he had seen the horse. They reached the point where the shadow had appeared, thinking that they had just seen a real horse and rider. However, all thoughts that this was the case disappeared when they reached the bridge where the bushes stopped: between the end of the bushes and the brickwork of the bridge there was only a very small gap, barely big enough for a person to squeeze through, and definitely not big enough for a large horse. At this point the two were very frightened, as they realized that they had seen a ghost, and they ran all the way home.

Stuart tells me that there is a local legend of the ghostly horse and rider told by villagers, and that others have seen him. His appearance gives the impression that he is injured, and maybe his distress has left an imprint in time destined to be repeated again and again.

This story has all the indications of a recording type of haunting, by far the most common of all in my investigations. Somehow the horse and rider have had their actions in life frozen in time, to be played back to anyone sensitive enough to tune in.

CASE 11 | A BAG OF CHERRIES

RECOUNTING HER story to me over a cup of coffee, Wendy M was still a little overcome by the vividness of her experience – the experience of seeing and actually touching a ghost. She is a mother of nine children, and a collector of delicate blue-and-white porcelain which adorns two large dressers in her lounge. Her story, the details of which will always be etched firmly on her mind, is at once touching and a little sad.

Wendy's paternal grandmother died when she was about eight years old. None of the family was too upset, as they did not get on very well and had seen little of her over the preceding years. It was quite a shock, however, when Wendy M, who was about 12, arrived home from school one afternoon to find her grandmother sitting on a cane chair in the living room. Her sister had come home slightly earlier and was upstairs changing out of her school uniform.

Wendy can remember asking her grandmother where her mum was. She replied, 'In the kitchen dear, getting tea ready.' Wendy, who had at this point almost forgotten that the old lady was dead, said, 'You haven't been to see us for ages', to which her grandmother replied, 'No, I know, but I thought I would bring you these.' She stood up, walked towards her granddaughter and handed her a brown paper bag full of cherries. Wendy can remember actually touching the woman's hand and the bag of cherries, which were juicy and ripe, a real luxury in those days. It all felt very real and solid. As Wendy went to eat a cherry from the bag, her grandmother said, 'No, run upstairs and get out of your uniform; you know what your mother's like about that.' So she ran upstairs and quickly changed, returning downstairs within minutes.

Her mother was busy laying the table for tea, but her grandmother was not there. She asked her mother where the old lady was, but was told, 'You know she doesn't get home until after six.' (Her maternal grandmother at that time lived with the family and worked locally as a housekeeper.) Wendy got cross and replied, 'No, Grandma Piddington.' Wendy can still remember how angry her mother was on hearing that remark, and also how baffled. She told the child that grandmother Piddington could not possibly have been in the house, as she was dead and buried years ago. The bag of cherries was nowhere to be seen either. Wendy was sent to bed and told not to make up such wicked stories again.

After spending the rest of the day and night hungry and sulking under the bedcovers, she had ample time to reflect on the encounter. It seemed so amazing to the child, as the woman and the bag of cherries had been so real and solid, even though the old lady had been dead for four years at the time.

Such an incident occurring so early in her life has led Wendy to question how we perceive this life and also death. Since then, she has had other 'odd', inexplicable experiences and says that she has at last come to accept them all as being part of a larger picture. As she told me, in her opinion some people just seem to be more sensitive to such things. After all, it was only she who saw her grandmother that day. It would seem to have given her some hope and belief in an afterlife – maybe even one that overlaps and at times infringes upon our own, albeit fleetingly.

Wendy is not alone in seeing a close deceased relative once after death. I have many times been contacted with such stories. It appears to be a fortunate experience for the bereaved as it reassures them about a possible afterlife, making them in turn less afraid of their own death. This must always be a far healthier outlook to have. It is always foolish to fear the inevitable.

This was not Wendy's only paranormal experience, but it was to her the one that had the most meaning. This very busy mother tells me that she considers her psychic ability both a blessing and a curse. On the plus side, if anyone in her family is in imminent trouble she can usually warn them, or failing that at least be prepared. One time, Wendy's son was late back from town. She just knew that he had been arrested and was very worried. A couple of minutes later, she received a phone call from the local police station asking her to come and pick up her son. He had got into a fight and the police had arrested him.

On the other hand, sometimes it is quite unpleasant knowing about events before they happen and can be rather unnerving.

CASE 12 THE OLD WOMAN

IT WAS mid-July 1996 and I was asked to do a talk-show on Radio Northampton. It was to be the third such broadcast I had done that year, talking about my first book, some of the local cases I had covered, and my own experiences of hauntings in the Northamptonshire area. I took along with me a couple of friends, Paul and Sue Hopgood, whose experiences of sharing their home with a playful poltergeist I included in my first book. The radio interviewer, Jim, wanted to talk to them about their ghost (see Case 47).

As we sat drinking coffee together waiting to be called in to be interviewed, we all felt a little nervous as we were to be on 'live' radio. This is difficult, as you cannot afford to 'dry up' once on air and you can never be sure exactly what questions you will be asked. In my experience the media are always very sceptical about the paranormal, although they love featuring programmes on the matter as there is such a lot of public interest. Waiting with us in the studio was a lady called Elsie who had reportedly seen a UFO some years before, and, as she had just written a book, had been invited to discuss the incident.

A young radio assistant first noticed that the studio had suddenly become very cold. Indeed it was so chilly that Elsie had begun to shiver. I joked to the two women working at the radio station that the air-conditioning was a bit fierce – it was an extremely hot day. One replied that they had no air-conditioning. We were then called in one by one to discuss the Northamptonshire ghosts featured in my book and the fact that I was working on a sequel. As is usual with many radio programmes, after the show listeners are invited to phone in with their stories and any questions they want to ask those interviewed. I was given some headphones and sat by a switchboard waiting for calls.

The last time I had been on radio the response had been very good and I hoped for the same again, but to everyone's dismay the switchboard and phonelines all went dead. No-one calling in could hear me speak and all I could hear were lots of odd clicks and whistling noises. Jim, the presenter, joked that maybe Paul and Sue's poltergeist (Fred) had followed them to the studio and had decided to disrupt the show. The subsequent programme, which I believe was a gardening phone-in, had to be cancelled, as the lines would not work properly after our departure.

Paul and Sue Hopgood with a selection of their amulets and power eggs.
They are talented mediums, who have turned their work into an art form.

For two days after our visit, the radio station experienced an icy cold draught in one of the studios, the source of which was not discovered, and the phones and switchboard continued to be faulty. The presenters made plenty of references on air to the 'spook' that had invaded the radio station.

The following week I visited Paul and Sue and told them about the radio station's two days of chaos after the show featuring us. Paul told me he was not at all surprised and explained why: he is a medium and said that on entering the building, which is situated in the heart of Northampton town centre, he felt it to be haunted by the spirit of an elderly lady who used to live there. He believes that the very subject of the programme featured that day, and the fact that Jim was sceptical and scoffed at their poltergeist story, somehow angered and activated the spirit of the old woman residing there.

Since the events of that day, I have not been asked to go back and talk again at the radio station. I look forward to doing so and wonder if similar things would occur. Perhaps that is the very reason, however, why Paul, Sue and I have not been asked back.

CASE 13 ECHOES FROM THE PAST

VIV FROM Northampton has had several ghostly experiences. She told me that she is descended, on her mother's side of the family, from Spanish gypsies, and Viv believes that she herself is psychic. When she was a young child, the family lived in Hilldon in Germany in an armed-forces house. The house was large, being two buildings knocked through into one. It backed onto woodland and at the back of this were the ruins of a monastery. The family was large and so they needed the space provided by the house.

As long as she lived in Germany in this house, Viv suffered from nightmares and had the feeling that her home was haunted. The cellar door was a thick wooden one and many times Viv, her mother or sisters were down in the cellar when the door would slam and lock on its own, trapping them down there. One time one of Viv's sisters was pushed down the cellar steps and had the door slammed behind her; as she lay in the dark at the bottom of the steps, she saw a small light whizz past her ear, something like a lighted match. At first she was angry and scared, believing one of her family had cruelly pushed her, but when she was discovered and let out of the cellar, the family were all shocked as they had been nowhere near the girl at the time.

Sometimes the shadowy, cowled figure of a monk was seen walking through the rooms. This may have been some sort of recording from the past, considering the house's close proximity to the former monastery beyond the wood.

Viv's next odd experience happened when her mother was gravely ill in hospital. At the time, Viv was living in an art gallery in Wellingborough. She woke up suddenly at 4.20am in floods of tears.

Eventually she went back to sleep, only to be woken up later by her brother John on the phone. Their mother had died, and the time of her death was 4.20am, the exact time at which Viv had woken up in tears. She had always been her mother's favourite, being the youngest child.

At the present time, Viv is living in a Victorian house in the centre of Northampton. The ground the house is built on was formerly an orchard. Viv believes this house to be haunted by the old lady who used to live there. Before Viv moved in, the house had been empty for about five years. From the first day, odd things have happened in the house: lights are turned off and on by themselves, as is the central heating – much to Viv's annoyance, especially during hot weather. Small household items go missing, only to turn up later in unexpected places. Viv's cat is often distressed by the ghost and stares up at a spot on the ceiling on the upstairs landing; strangely enough, her two German Shepherd dogs are not worried.

Some clue to the identity of the restless spirit haunting the house (if, indeed, that is what it is), was provided by a neighbour. Apparently the previous owner of the property was a reclusive old lady who had very little to do with her neighbours. She collapsed and died one day in the kitchen. Maybe she has never left. The house certainly still holds on to her personality in some way, and I am very glad I do not live there myself.

Viv, of course, must feel it acutely, owing to her heightened psychic ability. People living in houses haunted in this way often report feeling like an intruder in their own homes. This is a feeling which many find distressing, and they have to move.

CASE 14 # MOVING CLOSER

IT WAS spring 1997 when I went to Angela's home to read her palm and do her tarot cards. She lived on the outskirts of Northampton in a modern brick-built house. The young woman greeted me nervously, a bit unsure of what was to come.

We both sat down at her kitchen table and I sensed a great sadness surrounding her. Despite her smiling, pretty face and friendly, cheerful attitude, I could sense that this dark-haired young woman had suffered in life. I took her hand, studying its lines and patterns. One of the first things I picked up about her was that she had Irish ancestry, and she confirmed that she did, on her mother's side. Sadly, though, her mother had died. I also felt that she had a sister with whom she was extremely close, despite their differences. Angela said she was a twin.

Then, when I looked to see how many children she'd had, I saw signs that she had lost one child. This is not an uncommon feature to see on a hand, as many women miscarry. However, such a thing is always difficult to say, for the simple reason that one may be wrong. Angela then told me that she had lost a little girl at birth; she told me all about her, how pretty she had been and how perfect. Although it had happened a few years before, there were tears in her voice as she talked about it.

Angela fetched a small decorative box from the next room, opened the lid and took out a tiny photograph of the baby. The hospital had dressed the baby and taken her picture. The child looked asleep, tiny and doll-like, and very like her mother. It was so sad; as a mother myself, I really felt for Angela and how she had suffered. She told me after a while that it had been difficult to talk about her loss.

It seems that people often give you just so much time to mourn, and after that they somehow expect you to get on with life as before, keeping quiet about it and pushing the whole thing to the back of your mind. I feel that this has a lot to do with our Western culture and fear of death and the unknown beyond it. We have so many euphemisms for death and the dying process, it is as if we will do almost anything but mention the dreaded word itself. Perhaps by not mentioning it outright we think we can protect ourselves from the reality of our own mortality. This is wrong, and I believe ultimately unhealthy. Other countries and cultures have different views on this subject. They face death with more of a sense of reality, even taking care of their own relatives prior to burial by washing and preparing the corpse themselves. They seem to be less afraid of death.

As we spoke together about the baby, Angela began to shiver. The kitchen had become very cold, and we both sensed the presence of another person or persons there. I was unsure at first who or what it was, but quickly came to realize that it was Angela's mother and her child. Possibly they had been attracted to the house by the strong emotions exhibited that morning. I told Angela that I felt that the two of them were together. Within minutes the atmosphere changed and the room slowly warmed up.

We sat and chatted for a while about other aspects of Angela's life, the future and what it could hold. When I left the house, around lunchtime, I felt emotionally drained, but hoped that the young woman had taken some comfort from the contact with her loved ones.

CASE 15 THE VEGETABLE PLOT

ANNE-MARIE is an excellent mobile hairdresser who often comes to our home. She is always bubbly and cheerful, and had grown up in the same Northamptonshire village as I did. On hearing that I had just completed a book on the subject of ghosts, she half-joked to me that her own house might be haunted. I had been there a couple of times on social visits, but only downstairs. It was, she told me, the upstairs master bedroom that was haunted.

She asked me, as she cut my hair, if I could pop round next time I was in the village and have a look upstairs myself, to see if I could psychically pick up anything useful. Apparently, one night Anne-Marie had woken up. In the semi-darkness, she saw a stooped figure looking at her in bed. She was terrified, and hoping that she was just dreaming she closed her eyes tight. Then, having dared to reopen them, she saw a dark, eerie shadow standing near to the wardrobe. Her boyfriend woke up and saw it too. However, as he is quite a sceptic, he dismissed it as just another shadow. Anne-Marie told me that one of her two little boys has also seen it.

A few days later, I visited their house, unsure of what to expect – was it a haunting? It could have been one of the 'recording' type of phenomena, therefore totally harmless and no more real than an image on a television screen.

I went to the back door and looked out over the very long back garden, with its lawn full of children's toys, abandoned for the moment but ready to be picked up and played with anew later. I knocked, and Anne-Marie let me in, cheerful as ever. She told me some more about the ghost while making us both a drink.

We both went upstairs. The house is set on a steep hill overlooking old farm buildings and arable farmland. It was pleasantly decorated inside, and the atmosphere was also very pleasant. I didn't expect to pick up any feelings of a ghost. We went into the master bedroom, which contained a bed, a wardrobe and a chest-of-drawers.

I sat on the bed, trying to concentrate. Then I felt the presence of a sad man. He walked into the room; the temperature dropped and I felt cold. Then I heard the old man say, 'This is my house. I didn't have a wardrobe there. There is for the dressing table. They have dug up all my vegetables. I've lost them all.' Then, after pausing briefly, he said, 'Why was there a baby in the bed?'

I told Anne-Marie all this, and she was a little shocked. At the end of the garden, now grassed over, she had found the suggestion of a previous vegetable plot, with a few roots and shoots still present. She promised to restore it to its former glory. Also, she hadn't told me that on the night she saw the ghost one of her small boys had naughtily crept into his parents' bed. The old man had noticed this and disapproved.

I tried to communicate with him, telling him to go forward and leave this place in peace. It belonged to others now. He had to go, as he was scaring two lovely little boys, and it wasn't nice or fair. I waited for some moments; then we all went downstairs for a cup of tea.

I do hope the matter is resolved and the former tenant of this house can leave this young family in peace at last.

CASE 16 AFTER THE SÉANCE

AFTER HEARING wine expert John Hawes talking on Radio Northampton about his frightening experience during a séance and its repercussions, I was keen to interview him myself. It was a rainy afternoon in June 1998 when we met outside the church gates in the village of Woodford near Kettering.

John had explained to me over the phone that his story involved the church, and thought it better that we should meet up there. John had arranged with the vicar that we could have the keys. (The church has to be kept locked to prevent possible theft and vandalism.) We ran quickly from our cars towards the church, trying to dodge the heavy rain.

John opened the heavy oak door and we went inside. The church is an extremely beautiful old building, and despite the cloudy day light poured in through the stained-glass windows, flooding the interior with a myriad of colours. We sat down on a pew, halfway down on the left, and John related his remarkable story to me. His memory was sharp and seemingly undiminished despite the passage of time.

On a Saturday evening in 1964, John and a friend were having a drink at the White Horse pub at Lowick (it has since been renamed). Here they met two spiritualists who were recounting a ghostly incident at Fotheringay. John told me that at that time he was a complete sceptic on anything paranormal. He mocked the two strangers, saying that he totally disbelieved in ghosts. He thought the whole thing absolute nonsense.

Laughing, the two drinkers challenged the spiritualists to offer them proof. They decided to hold a séance in the pub after closing time, and with the permission of the landlord they did. They constructed a makeshift Ouija board on the table, using cut-out paper letters and an upturned wineglass. Having dimmed the lights, the four men sat round in a circle and in turn asked the Ouija board questions.

The glass moved about the table freely and both John and his disbelieving mate suspected the spiritualists of moving it. They voiced their suspicions and the two agreed to be blindfolded as a test. The letters were shuffled so that the two men had no idea of the sequence. The men told the two sceptics to ask questions that only they knew the answers to, to rule out any possibility of trickery.

John posed a question that at that time even he didn't know the answer to. He knew of the human heart that was interred at his local church in Woodford, although he was unsure of the name of the man to whom it once belonged. So he asked the Ouija, 'To whom does the heart in Woodford church belong?' The glass spelt out the letters T, R and A, and then cracked. With this, the atmosphere in the pub suddenly went very cold. John was very frightened, and left in a hurry, riding his motorbike home at great speed, as if the devil himself was giving chase.

Next day, still shaken by the events of the night before, he visited the rector at his local church and asked him about the heart kept in St Mary's church. The rector said that the heart was believed to be at least 700 years old and had been discovered during restoration work in the 1800s. Workmen had uncovered it when they removed a stone from an interior archway. A wrapped linen bundle fell out onto the floor and a small bamboo box spilled out its contents: a perfectly preserved, if somewhat blackened, human heart. They carefully picked it up, placed it back in the box and wrappings, and put it back in its original position.

The organ is thought to belong to a knight crusader who was killed in battle. He was buried in the country of his demise, but his heart was removed and brought back home for burial in his birthplace (apparently this was fairly common practice at the time). The rector then told John that the heart was thought to belong to either a Richard or a Walter Trayli. When the rector spelt out the name of the knight, John felt an involuntary cold shiver at the first three letters of the surname: T, R, A. The same letters had been spelt out by the glass the night before.

About three weeks later, John noticed in a local paper a photo of the interior of that church. It showed a kneeling, robed figure before the altar, not unlike a monk, or a person wearing a long pale robe or cloak. The head wasn't visible as the figure was bent forward. Apparently, when Gordon Carol, a teenager from Northampton, took the photo, he was alone in the church and saw nothing. The photo became quite a talking point among the villagers, as might be expected.

A couple of weeks after this, John and his mate once again went for a drink at the White Horse pub. To their surprise, the two spiritualists were back there too. The men struck up a conversation. The spiritualists told the two men that they believed strongly that their séance had disturbed the spirit of the knight Trayli, and that it could well account for the appearance of the ghost in the photograph at Woodford. They felt that they had reminded the knight of his untimely death. The two spiritualists suggested they hold a second séance in an attempt to discover more.

Both John and his drinking partner declined. They were much too scared to dabble again in what had hitherto been to them the unknown realm of ghosts and spirits – a world they really did not want to encounter any more.

As John and I sat quietly in the church, he told me that on Halloween 1982 the story of the Woodford ghost and the photo were shown on American television to an audience of 75 million viewers. Indeed, that photograph is very famous; it also appears in several of the books on the paranormal that I keep at home. A copy of the newspaper article and photograph are pinned up on the noticeboard at the back of the church.

As we sat talking, we both heard a metallic tinkling sound, a bit like a handbell, coming from the area of the vestry. I assumed at first that it it was the vicar preparing for Sunday service the next day. John turned to me, and I was surprised at how pale he looked. We both said, almost in unison, 'Did you hear that?' Maybe it was my imagination, but the temperature seemed to drop by a couple of degrees. There was a heaviness to the air, such as occurs before a thunderstorm, and I felt a kind of sleepy sensation of time standing still.

The noise continued at regular intervals, so I went off in search of its source, still half-suspecting someone hidden from our view at the back of the church, either on legitimate business or up to some sort of prank. I opened up the wrought-iron gates near to the altar and walked through. I heard the noise again, even clearer this time. I asked, 'Is there anybody there?' There wasn't. I had a good look around and, unsure of what to do next, I asked, 'If you can hear me, make that noise again.' We both heard the familiar tinkling sound reply.

Then I turned to face John, who was now sitting in the section of pews in the middle of the church. Briefly, from the corner of my eye, I glimpsed a tall, grey-cloaked figure pass to my left. I spun around to get a better look, but the figure was gone. Not quite believing my eyes, I asked my companion if he had seen it too, but he seemed in shock. He told me that he had seen enough, and wanted to leave right away. As I approached him, I noticed a strange area of dense shadow immediately to his left. He saw it too, and literally jumped to his feet. The shadow was exactly like the image that I had seen near the vestry.

After this, we both left the building, although I was keen to stay on a while. I felt quite excited as I could hardly believe what we had just witnessed. I had never expected anything out of the ordinary to happen on that wet June afternoon. Indeed, as I have stressed previously, in most cases nothing does. Anyone searching for ghosts usually finds them frustratingly elusive.

We both walked quickly from the church, grateful that the heavy summer rain had eased up slightly. When we described to each other the details of the shadowy grey figure, I realized that we had seen the same thing. It reminded us both of a snippet of black-and-white film.

John kindly invited me back to his house for a fortifying cup of tea. Here I met his wife, a very charming, down-to-earth woman who at first disbelieved our tale. She told me quite firmly that she regularly did the church flowers, and even when alone there had never felt afraid. She had never heard or seen anything untoward either.

As the three of us sat around the dining table, sipping tea and eating lemon spongecake, the conversation progressed, and I felt John's wife becoming more and more eager to believe us. We looked through a selection of books on the history of the village, and found an important clue in a very old, leatherbound book. Mention was made of a small brass bell that in the past was rung during the service of holy communion.

I felt a little concerned for John, as he seemed badly shaken up by his experience. Just as I was leaving, he told me that what had happened had brought back vivid memories of the incident 34 years earlier. He had felt the same cold shiver.

CASE 17 A PSYCHIC ASSAULT

REVEREND PHILIP Steff, who lives in the city of Bath, wrote to me in June 1998 to tell me of some of his own incredible experiences, and about some of the many people he has helped in his particular specialized ministry of exorcism. He is an ordained minister and also an experienced medium. I shall relate just one of his cases here.

One evening in July, Philip was contacted by a Mrs Katherine Baker, who was very concerned for her twin sons. Dean and Adrian, aged 23, were both quite ill. Dean, who was 2m (6ft) tall, presently weighed a mere 44kg (7 stone), as he found it almost impossible to eat. The other twin, Adrian, was showing signs of disturbance, which included memory loss and suspected heart problems.

Katherine claimed that her sons were both suffering the result of a satanic attack inflicted on them many months previously. It had occurred while the family had been living in America. Apparently a group of satanists had tried to recruit the boys into the group. When they refused, the satanists had cursed them. Whether it was just a coincidence or not (psychologists have found that even a belief in a curse can have detrimental physical and psychological effects), things just seemed to go wrong for the family from then on.

The father, who was a chef, became bankrupt, and at the same time the two boys' health began to suffer. They underwent a series of medical tests that proved inconclusive. The mother also admitted to Reverend Steff that when her boys were much younger she had messed about with a Ouija board. She wondered if this had somehow opened a door, leaving them all vulnerable to attack from negative forces.

Katherine Baker, who was living with her family in Lancashire, seemed in desperate need of help, and so Reverend Steff promised to visit them to perform an exorcism. He also decided to take along with him two assistants, Barbara and David Mellor, fellow ministers in the church of the Corinthians, who were, like himself, practising mediums. The three of them set out for Lytham St Anne's. When they arrived at the Bakers' home, they were met at the door by Katherine. Her face showed relief at the sight of them, and hopeful anticipation that her lengthy ordeal would soon be over.

Their host had cooked them a splendid meal, and they all sat down to enjoy it. It seemed that no sooner had they done that than the psychic assault began. In the room there came the stench of human excrement. It was so strong and unmistakable that quite understandably Barbara became nauseous. The three of them prayed and the awful smell disappeared.

They had decided to perform the exorcism on the following evening and so that first night, when all the others had retired, Philip sat up talking to Adrian and his sister. He told them about his work and beliefs and some of the many dozens of cases he had tackled over the years. Not all of them had been distressing; indeed there had been lighter moments that had proved quite amusing.

Suddenly Adrian got up, as he had sensed that his brother was under attack and in distress. Reverend Steff and the young man went upstairs into Dean's room. They placed a circle of salt around his bed as a form of protection.

Next day, Philip planned to perform the exorcism proper, and he had every hope of its success. He thought that he would need the additional help and positive energies of his two friends Barbara and David. While he and Barbara were waiting in the lounge, Philip glanced out of the window. As he did so, he sensed the presence of something evil in the room. They both saw a very black and shadowy form that took on the shape of a large bird. Philip commanded that the entity leave, and mentally projected the ghastly image departing from the room where the ceremony was to take place. When he turned round, he was shocked to see the impression that had been left upon the wall. It was the shape of a large bird, which had indented itself through the several layers of wallpaper, presumably when it departed.

Not deterred from his task, Philip began to set up the room in preparation at 5pm. The three ministers covered the dining table with a white cloth, and lit two white candles on either side of a consecrated wooden cross. Each member of the family was told to wear a cross that had been blessed with holy water. The three ministers recited the Lord's prayer and entreated the demons to leave the twins in peace. The service was concluded with a blessing.

Apparently the exorcism was entirely successful. Indeed, almost immediately afterwards Dean felt hungry and was able for the first time in ages to eat and enjoy a meal, something that would previously have been impossible for him as he had completely lost his appetite. The only evidence of the ordeal that the twins had been subjected to were the scars on their backs from lacerations that had mysteriously appeared.

Reverend Philip Steff has been working with those unfortunates believed to be possessed, and also in the 'clearance' of haunted properties, since 1979. He is sure of the reality of negative harmful entities and that psychic attack can be very real. Personally, I retain an open mind on such matters, as I know that the power of the mind can be very strong. Curses seem to exert a power over us only if we believe in them. If this belief is strong, then the mind on its own has the power to cause psychosomatic illness. The stronger the belief, the more powerful can be the hold on the body, and consequently the more severe the illness. This effect has been noted with stigmatics (those who exhibit physical wounds similar to those of Jesus Christ on the cross). Most of them show a wound through the palm, as indeed this is where the nails are shown to have been driven in icons and statues of Christ. However, historians have found that the nails would have been driven through the wrists of those crucified. Therefore the fervently religious stigmatics portray the wounds where they *believe* they would have been rather than where they *actually* would have been. I feel that this phenomenon shows the effect of a type of 'curse' that sufferers inflict on themselves in an attempt to empathize with Christ.

The case related above was reported in the magazine *Psychic News*, and also in local newspapers. The work of Reverend Philip Steff has also been shown on television. Other cases he has covered include the apparition of a former teacher in a school, and the possession by a malevolent entity of a medium that he knew.

STONE TAPE RECORDINGS

MANY GHOSTLY encounters fall into this category. They consist of re-enactments of past events, either auditory (noises from the past, such as bangs, talking or music) or visual (people long since dead repeating various actions that they did in life). Many paranormal researchers and scientists believe that some events and noises can be captured and recorded, rather in the way video cameras and tape-recorders do, to be replayed later. Maybe the very stones and bricks in the 'haunted' location can somehow do this, and when a 'trigger' comes along, such as a sensitive person who psychically tunes in, the recording is played and they are able to see and hear past events. In this way, the ghost that the person sees is no more real than a dead film star is when viewed in one of their films.

At the present time, how images can be recorded by buildings and the environment to be played back later is not fully understood. Small amounts of quartz are found naturally in brick and stone: quartz is used in clocks, computers and recording tape. The Earth is also one huge mag-net and electrical fields surround us all. Separately, therefore, it would appear that we have all the components we need to record such events. The only thing left that we need is a trigger to switch on the recording and a viewer or listener to witness or hear it. Someone with a heightened psy-chic awareness could be the ideal trigger, and viewer, in such a process.

If the stone tape recording theory was able to explain the appear-ance of *all* ghosts, then the idea of life beyond death as an explanation for ghostly phenomena could perhaps be discounted. However, this is clearly not the case.

Practitioners of the art of psychometry, who claim to be able to touch an object and read from it all about its history and that of its owner, are possibly exploiting such stone tape recording. They would suggest that strong thoughts and emotions can leave an imprint on an object or place that can be picked up at a later date.

Recording-type ghosts could also be termed 'anniversary hauntings', in that in many cases they appear regularly at the same time and on the same date year after year. Some writers on the paranormal have even compiled a list of locations in the British Isles where ghost-hunters can go on specific days and hope to strike lucky.

If we could understand more fully the mechanism by which stone tape recording works, the potential is terrific. Historians could go to ancient ruins and, under controlled conditions, trigger off a mini re-enactment of events in that location – maybe events that occurred centuries earlier. History could literally come alive before our eyes.

CASE 18 RAINING DOWN STONES

DEVON MUST surely be one of the most beautiful parts of the British Isles. The dramatic, unspoilt landscape with its historic stone buildings has inspired poets and writers for centuries. It was in one of these old granite buildings that Debbie, now a mother of three, was to experience the ghostly echoes of the past – a past that had not been totally forgotten and the effects of which would influence those living in the old former coaching inn, now called Northcoate Manor, to the present day.

The young Debbie was working as a groom for her cousin, who owned the small estate. Northcoate Manor is situated on the old London–Penzance coaching route. At the time Debbie worked there as a live-in groom, it had long ceased to be a coaching inn, and had become a very spacious family home. There had always been speculation regarding one of the fields at the rear of the house, next to a stream. In the deeds of Northcoate Manor, it was stipulated that the field was to be left untouched. It was left fallow, and used for grazing horses.

Debbie had heard stories of a doctor who lived at Northcoate Manor at the turn of the century. He had obviously not been the most successful of clinicians, as he apparently used the bottom field to bury all his mistakes. It was not known how many bodies were buried there, but it was thought to be more than a handful.

The ghostly goings-on at Northcoate Manor, however, centred not around this cemetery but on the house and its sweeping gravel driveway. At roughly the same time each year, near Christmas, footsteps were heard scrunching loudly up the gravel drive approaching the front door. When the door was opened, no-one was seen, except for one occasion when a man dressed in a long dark cloak and a hat was briefly glimpsed. This appears to have been some sort of recording from the past, as does Debbie's next encounter.

It was late one night and Debbie was settling down to sleep. Her bedroom was one of many in the large house, and it faced others across the upstairs landing. One of the owners' dogs began to howl loudly, and the room suddenly became very cold. Then she heard the footsteps of a woman walking along the corridor. This was accompanied by the sound of a long skirt swishing along the floor, which Debbie described as sounding like a character from an old black-and-white film with long crinoline skirts. The noise was very distinctive, and Debbie was very frightened by it, as she knew everyone was in bed and long since asleep.

In the morning, Debbie's cousin's mother and father, who slept in one of the bedrooms along the other side of the corridor, said that they had also heard the mystery woman, and not for the first time. An older daughter of the couple, who also lived in the house, had become so afraid of the noisy activities of the ghost that she refused to sleep alone in her room, even though she was in her thirties.

Talking about her experiences in Devon brought back a memory from childhood that Debbie had almost forgotten. She was nine years old, and was visiting her older sister, who lived at Streetly, near Sutton Coldfield. The wood at the end of Egerton Road was a dark and unfriendly place, and the young Debbie was told that local people rarely went there. One day, the temptation became too much, and the little girl went for a walk inside the wood. It was then that she became pelted by small stones. The rain of stones was persistent, and they appeared to come from nowhere. At the time, unable to understand the attack, Debbie assumed it to be the result of birds dropping the missiles from above. She said they just came 'zinging through the trees' at her, and as no-one else was about it was puzzling. It was not until recently, when Debbie saw a programme about a poltergeist and its stone-throwing antics, that she wondered if just such a force could have been at work.

CASE 19 DYCHURCH LANE

MURDER, OWING to the very nature and brutality of the act, that is the robbing of someone else's life, can be the cause of a subsequent haunting, either at the crime scene itself or where the victim is buried. Case histories about apparitions of murder victims abound and often become local legends.

Just off Northampton town centre is a quiet back street called Dychurch Lane. It is a cobbled street. On one side are the backs of some shops, and on the other are the fenced-off gardens of tall houses, many of which are now used as offices. In the lane are a few large over-stuffed dustbins, spilling their rubbish onto the street.

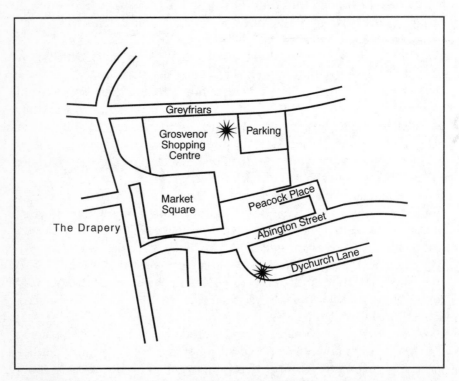

Northampton town centre, showing the Grosvenor Centre (see Case 44) and Dychurch Lane. The two places where ghosts have been seen are marked with asterisks.

These uneven cobbles are the same ones onto which Annie Prichard's blood gushed when she was killed and dismembered there over 100 years ago. After her head had been hacked off, the poor woman's remains were bundled into a sack and discarded like unwanted rubbish. Annie's ghost is believed to haunt Dychurch Lane to this day, her blood long since washed from the cobblestones. Local people still sometimes encounter Annie's ghost there even though she was apparently buried in East Haddon Cemetery.

Dychurch Lane, looking towards Fish Street.

This story is probably as famous a murder to the people of Northampton as those of 'Jack the Ripper' are to the people of London. Such a horrific act cannot and should not be forgiven, and is the stuff of which legends are made. It is not uncommon for murder scenes to be haunted by the victim for many years afterwards. Strong emotion leaves its own kind of fingerprint.

CASE 20 THE GLOWING HAND

THE FOLLOWING case was related to me by twin brothers Gavin and Lance Rixson, whose family home is at Walton-le-Dale in Preston. They moved into the house in December 1988, when the twins were 16 years old.

The house is over 200 years old and is near to the area where the Battle of Preston was fought in 1649. Whether this has any bearing on the paranormal activity in the Rixsons' house is unclear. However, ghostly activity on and around the sites of old battlegrounds is not uncommon and much has been written on the subject. Both of the twins have experienced odd goings-on, and find an explanation of it all elusive.

The first thing that happened when the family moved in was a series of odd thumping sounds that seemed to come from within the walls themselves. It was hard to pinpoint which part of the room they were coming from. Strange shadows were also seen, of what appeared to be objects floating across the bedrooms at night before disappearing. Once, Gavin saw what looked like an old-fashioned curtain rail on the wall above his bed. Such a curtain rail did not exist in the room and he was forced to conclude that he was witnessing some sort of vision from the past.

The most frightening thing to occur happened one night at about 3.30am. Gavin woke with a jolt to see a strange, hand-like shape, which was emitting a green glow, hovering above his bed for a few seconds. Immediately afterwards, he felt an overwhelming presence and a sense of sadness in the room.

Thankfully, the nightly visitations have lessened somewhat, but the twins have told me that occasionally things are still seen in the house.

However, all the family have become used to the goings-on and no longer jump out of bed to turn on the lights. They have tried to think of a rational explanation for the odd events, but have not been able to come up with one.

Since writing to me, the family concerned have become almost blasé about the odd events in their home. This case has all the hallmarks of a recording, and as such the family is correct not to be afraid. The best thing for them to do is catalogue all the visions and look for any patterns that may be revealed. Recording-type hauntings sometimes fade gradually, worn away slowly by time like a photograph that fades.

A MEMENTO OF SCOTLAND

CASE 21

SUE WAS on holiday in the early 1990s, and she visited St Salvator's Chapel in St Andrews, Scotland. Famous for its royal and ancient golf club, St Andrews boasts buildings of a beautiful golden and grey stone, much of which was taken from the original cathedral. While visiting the chapel, Sue took some photographs of the interior and the altar. She was struck at the time by the gloomy atmosphere of the place. When she returned home and had the photographs developed, she was surprised to see a misty, white figure in front of the altar in one of her pictures. Sue said no-one was standing there at the time that she took the photograph.

Unfortunately, as the photograph is now a few years old and has faded, I felt unable to include it in this book. It would not stand up very well to reproduction and the negative, sadly, has been mislaid. It is a considerable shame in cases when photographic evidence is poor. A chance is then missed for a piece of the puzzle to be put into place. For example, if a reliable witness reports a sighting in the presence of other reliable witnesses, and has a photo showing what he alleges they have seen, it is hard to refute. Such evidence is extremely rare, but does happen on occasion. Researchers into the paranormal must always search for such evidence, and to them it is a little like the holy grail.

CASE 22 WAITING AT THE STATION

BRISTOL PARKWAY station is the setting for the event that occurred on St Valentine's Day, 14 February, in 1996. It was a cold evening, and Linda was waiting on the station platform for her fiancé Simon's train to arrive from Derbyshire. It was getting late, and Linda was alone except for another young girl standing a little further along the platform. Bored with waiting and a little cold, Linda tentatively wondered about striking up a conversation with the girl.

Just then the train pulled into the station and Linda greeted Simon with a hug. As they walked slowly from the platform towards the car park, Linda noticed the girl, who looked rather sad, walking in the same direction. Laughing to Simon, Linda joked, 'Oh dear, the poor girl must have been stood up,' and looked at her fiancé with a smile. She was taken aback, because Simon could not see the girl at all, even though she was only about 1 m (3 ft) away from them. Simon then lightheartedly teased Linda that she must have seen a ghost.

When Linda looked back at the spot where seconds before the young girl had stood, the car park was completely empty; the girl had vanished without a trace. The couple searched around them for some minutes, totally mystified.

To this day, Linda is absolutely sure of what she saw. The girl was young and dressed in contemporary clothing of denim jeans and jacket. Her appearance was totally normal, not transparent or odd-looking. Her behaviour had been one of some anxiety while waiting for the train and she did seem sad. All the time she had been jangling and fiddling with her keys.

This case proves that often ghosts appear so lifelike and solid that the real shock comes later when the observer realizes that he or she has just seen a ghost. These types of totally solid and real apparitions can be even more shocking to the observer than a misty, half-seen spectre, for the simple reason that it is more of a shock when they disappear.

I saw one of this type myself some years ago. There was a woman standing by my garden gate. I tried to approach and have a conversation with her, but she was gone before I had chance to open my mouth. It was then that I slowly realized that the woman I had seen was long since dead and simply could not have been there.

NOTHING TO BE SCARED OF

CASE
23

TELLA DEMETRIOU from Cyprus wrote telling me about her long-running experiences of seeing the spirit of her grandmother. Stella lives in the fishing town of Limassol in Cyprus; it is a very ancient fishing town and now also a popular tourist centre. The hotels fan out along the sandy coast and, because of the wonderful sunny climate enjoyed by the island, are busy all year round.

For a long time, Stella had felt a presence in her house, but only when she was alone. It felt as if someone was passing by or watching her, but it was never frightening or sinister. As she is an antiques lover, in 1995 Stella brought some pieces of furniture to Cyprus from Denmark, a 1905 Larsen piano among them. One night, while sitting in the next room to where the piano was, she felt the presence very strongly once again. Turning her head towards the next room, she saw a tall female figure; it was like a kind of colourless shadow, but a recognizable one. It was Stella's grandmother, wearing a long dress and scarf, with her hair styled in the usual way. The ghost approached the recently acquired piano and passed her hand over it, almost as if to express her approval. Then she left. The incident was only the first of many to come.

Stella and her British friend Barbara were chatting one night when Barbara turned to her friend and exclaimed, 'I don't mean to scare you or anything, but a ghost is sitting next to you.' As Stella was by that time very used to her grandmother's presence, she just smiled and asked Barbara to describe the ghost. Unsurprisingly, the description matched exactly that of her dead grandmother.

Stella tells me that she often feels the presence of the old lady in her house, but is very happy knowing that she is always at her side. Stella's experiences of her grandmother's presence still being felt long after her death are fairly common. Many have felt the presence of their deceased close relatives, especially in the early weeks. When my own grandmother died, when I was small, I can remember wondering why everyone was sad. I somehow knew that she was with us, not in any solid sense as she had been when alive, but more like tiny droplets in the air. It helped me considerably at the time to come to terms with her death. She had died in great suffering but now was released, and for the first time in my life I realized that part of ourselves goes on after our death.

Whether this is the 'soul', or the essence of our personality, something of each individual remains.

CASE 24 THE MORGUE

IF ONE subscribes at all to the stone tape recording theory, then presumably any place with a predominance of stone in its construction is a likely place to see ghosts or hear sounds from the past.

It was in about 1990 that I was holidaying with my family on the island of Jersey in the English Channel, a beautiful, green and rock-strewn island that is more like coastal France than England, with a warm, dry climate.

It was halfway through the holiday and, keen to see all the sights of the island, we visited the underground hospital. This is situated in a series of huge caves. It was artificially constructed during the Second World War and resembles a rabbit warren. Its sheer size, when you consider that it was hewn by hand, is quite amazing.

During the Second World War, when the Germans captured the island, they took prisoners of war, Jews and some local people and set them to work building the hospital. Such a place was obviously safe from enemy attack, being many feet under the earth. It was used as a military hospital and centre of operations.

Today the place is a tourist attraction. Some of the rooms are kitted out as they would have been in the 1940s, complete with waxwork figures, furniture authentic to the period, and even sound-effects.

Apparently, many men died in the making of these tunnels, owing to exhaustion and rock falls, not to mention the German soldiers who died of their wounds in there. Anyone visiting the caves today can't help but feel the effects of this, and pick up its gloomy atmosphere. Maybe this atmosphere affected me and led directly to my vivid experience. It is hard to say, but I am not the only person to have had such an encounter in that place.

We were all walking along the central corridor in the caves. The children were not very interested in them. Becky, the youngest, was a bit scared as the tunnels are quite dark and smelled a little musty. We were part of the way along the corridor, and had seen inside some of the reconstructed rooms. We walked past some with bars in front of them; they had obviously been used to detain prisoners.

All of a sudden I felt extremely cold, unnaturally so, and felt a rush of freezing air run through my hair. Then, glancing to the left, I saw a sign above one room. It said 'Mortuary'. I saw a series of what looked suspiciously like bodies. Some were intact physically, but one had lost a leg. His clothes were ripped and he was covered in a fine layer of white dust. The smell of blood was unmistakable and overwhelming. I felt sick at this, initially thinking the room was yet another reconstruction, albeit one in bad taste. Then I realized that somehow, in some way, I was seeing the mortuary as it really had been during the war.

Leaving the children with my husband, I just ran and ran as fast as possible, wanting to get away from all those bodies and all that death. At the exit to the caves, an oldish woman was standing in a sort of booth, selling souvenirs of the hospital to the exiting tourists. The woman took one look at me and asked if I was all right. Breathlessly, I told her that I felt sick and that I had just seen the mortuary full of bodies.

She looked unsurprised at this, and remarked that of course the cave didn't have a reconstructed room like that, but the morgue had been where I described it. The woman told me that other visitors had seen this, and other strange things. Some had simply heard noises that frightened or intrigued them. It was all fairly common stuff, although she had never experienced any of it herself. It is not like me to be frightened of anything, but as I came out of the cave, despite the blazing heat of the midsummer sun, I was shivering.

<table>
<tr><td>C A S E</td><td rowspan="2"></td></tr>
<tr><td>25</td></tr>
</table>

TURNING ON THE SWITCH

WHENEVER I can, a few times a year at least, I endeavour to spend the night with recording equipment in some of the places that feature in my books. I spent such a night late in 1996 at the Spreadeagle pub in Piddington.

The village is just outside Northampton and it has a long history. On the outskirts of the village, among green fields, are the remains of a

Roman settlement, which was in its time probably much larger than the modern village that has taken its place. Once a year, teams of young archaeologists camp out in the fields of Piddington to uncover more of the precious remains. Previous finds have included a wonderful mosaic floor, and in 1995 a number of skeletons were found, one of a baby. At the end of the day the archaeologists descend on the only pub in the village, the Spreadeagle. Digging is thirsty work.

The landlord Dave told me that he had been a total disbeliever in ghosts until one night in about 1993, when he was locking all the doors after closing time. When he came to the toilet block, he saw the shadowy figure of a man behind the half-glazed door. Knowing the pub to be empty of customers, he shouted out gingerly, 'Who are you?' There was no reply and, on investigating, the figure had disappeared. Dave went up to bed very scared, as he knew that he had just seen a ghost. He told me that the figure was definitely that of a tallish man, but seemed more like a shadow than a solid being.

The landlady, Sheila his wife, has seen many odd things happen while clearing up in the bar area. She does not like to talk about the ghost. Trays of glasses move on their own and once while she was cleaning up a bottle smashed to pieces when no-one was near it.

Some of the older regulars said that many of the previous landlords had also encountered the ghost, who was known as Daniel. The names of all the landlords are written up on a framed list hung on the snooker-room wall, together with a brief history of the village and of the public house itself.

A few months after interviewing the staff and customers at the Spreadeagle, I asked Dave if I and a fellow researcher could mount a ghostwatch there one evening after closing time. He was a bit reluctant at first, but eventually agreed to it. The next week, Patrick and I, armed with two cameras, infrared film and a sensitive tape-recorder, arrived at the pub. It was dark and very cold.

The landlord showed us in, and after about half an hour of chatting went to bed. I set up the tape-recorder in the rear passageway where Dave had seen the ghost. I left it on and running. Then we loaded up the cameras, one with infra-red film, the other with ordinary film, and decided to base ourselves mainly in the lounge area, where a barmaid had seen the ghost (which she initially took to be a customer).

In all, we remained at the pub from midnight until 4am. Nothing much happened; or at least that was my impression at first. We saw no evidence of the famous but elusive Daniel. There was a considerable drop in temperature at one point, but we just put that down to the heating being turned down at night.

I wrote the ghostwatch off as a bit of a waste of time and an exercise in boredom and sleep deprivation. However, a couple of days later I suddenly remembered the tape-recorder that had been set up in the rear. I rewound the tape and played it back. Instead of an empty tape, I heard a series of funny clicking sounds, as if somebody was turning on and off a machine or electric light switch, or maybe even the recorder itself. We heard no such noise when we sat in the pub that night and I wonder if this could possibly be paranormal in origin.

Paul and Sue Hopgood, whose own house has experienced a long-running poltergeist outbreak, told me once that many times just prior to the activity they hear a click or knocking sound (they too have caught this on tape), a bit like someone turning on a machine. Perhaps there is a link here somewhere, another small piece of the jigsaw. It may be that paranormal activity requires a trigger that can be heard being activated. This is just a theory, but I always find coincidences interesting and worthy of possible further study.

CASE 26   DOPPELGÄNGER

ANNA C, a teenager, recently wrote to me telling me of her rather unsettling experience. Three months earlier she had briefly glimpsed the ghost of her mother.

Anna's parents had split up very acrimoniously and divorced. Anna had gone to live with her mother, but often spent her weekends with her father at the former family home. One particular weekend, on the Saturday evening, she was sitting on the sofa watching television. Her father had nipped out for a few minutes. Anna turned round and was shocked to see her mother curled up in the armchair, busily reading a book.

Blinking, totally disbelieving what she had just seen, as Anna knew that at that time her mother was at home several miles away, she looked again, but the image had gone. Anna was extremely frightened at this point, as she wondered with horror if her mother was dead, as surely only the dead could appear as ghosts.

She quickly ran to the phone and rang her mother's house, concerned that perhaps she had met with an accident. Her mother cheerfully answered the phone and assured her young daughter that she was fine.

Next day, when the girl returned home, she told her mother her reasons for her anxious phone call the evening before. Surprisingly, her mother was sitting reading at the time of her daughter's vision. She was thinking about Anna and reminiscing about her life in her former home.

Experiences such as these are far from uncommon. These apparitions of the living seem from my research on the subject to occur at times of great crisis either for the person who sees the apparition or for the one who appears. There were many similar cases reported during the Second World War. A large proportion were between mothers (at home) and sons (away fighting). Some were in the days or moments just before the son's death. The most often-used expression for this phenomenon is doppelgänger or 'double'.

Another possible trigger for this type of experience is two minds at the same moment thinking of the same familiar place and memories of it. I believe this to have been the case with Anna C and her mother. Both were apparently thinking at that time of each other and as a direct result the vision of the mother appeared in her previous home, sitting in her favourite chair doing what she often did in the evening, losing herself in a book. This series of thoughts brought about the teenager's clear vision of her mother. One can understand perhaps the young girl's shock on seeing the ghost, as we normally only associate them with the dead.

What could well be happening in such visions is one of two possible scenarios:

1   It is a type of very vivid telepathy between the viewer and the person projecting ('projector'). This involves strong emotions on the part of one or both parties, and usually requires also a strong bond between them. The projected image is thus a hallucination conjured up by the viewer, but probably sent by the projector.

2   It is a recording of the person seen as the apparition as a fixed image in time, made by the fabric of the building or (if outside) some process in the environment. Minutes, days or even years may elapse before it is witnessed. If one accepts that such a process could account for a proportion of ghost sightings, then there is obviously no rule that any person in the recording must be dead when it is played back to the viewer.

There are many superstitions worldwide tied up with this phenomenon. For example, in some countries it is said to be a bad portent to see oneself as a doppelgänger. If this occurs, then the experiencer is supposed to face death within a year. Of course, such superstitions are quite without any basis in fact.

CASE 27 | AT THE WORLD'S END

ONE OF the most haunted public houses that I have ever visited during the course of my investigations is the World's End at Ecton in Northamptonshire. Dating from 1645, It is a large and imposing building of attractive, local, yellow sandstone. Extensively refurbished in recent years, it is now strictly a family pub with a large downstairs children's play area and an impressive oak-beamed dining room, formerly a barn.

The current manageress, Belinda Blackmore, started work there in January 1998, and was ill-prepared for what she was to experience. She told me that the pub took its name from an incident connected with the battle of Naseby. The pub became the last resting place for many of the dead and wounded soldiers after the fighting. The dead were placed in the cellars before burial, and the wounded were patched up and rested before travelling down to London. For so many of these men, it was literally to be their last stop-off in this world, hence the name World's End.

It is rumoured that part of the pub's former grounds (now a playground for the children of the village of Ecton) became a mass burial site for these unfortunate soldiers. As you walk in through the central back entrance, above the inglenook fireplace you can see two armoured breastplates. If you then glance up to your immediate left, on a high recess in the wall there are two authentic metal soldiers' helmets, presumably left there after the battle and kept as souvenirs.

The World's End pub consists of several separate rooms downstairs and two roomy flats upstairs for staff members. However, most of the ghostly activity has occurred downstairs and in the two cellar rooms. A few years ago, the cellar floor was resurfaced, which resulted in the floor level being raised several inches above that of the original. Some time after this, a delivery man came running up the stairs from the cellar into the bar. He breathlessly told the staff that he had just seen a ghost. It was the ghost of a man who was seen from the knees up. The bottom halves of his legs were missing – presumably he was walking at the level of the old cellar floor. The delivery man was extremely shaken by his sighting and vowed never to go back down the cellar again, or at least not on his own. Indeed most of the present staff at the pub hate going down there on their own, feeling it to be very depressing and creepy, despite the fact that it is clean and well lit.

Adjacent to these cellars, and virtually at the same level, is the children's play area, consisting of two rooms filled with climbing equipment, ball pools, and walls painted with colourful cartoon characters. These rooms, Belinda told me, are permanently cold and prove virtually impossible to heat, even in summer.

It was on the staircase next to the playrooms that the manageress had her most unnerving experience. She was descending the stairs when she distinctly felt someone brush slowly past her. There was no-one else there at the time, and as she felt this touch she experienced a type of electric shock. She also heard a weird buzzing and crackling sound, like the sound of overhead electric power cables. The sensation was similar to a strong static shock. When she went back up the stairs, frightened, she was asked what on earth had happened, as apparently her short dark hair was standing on end. She also noticed that her arms were covered in goose-bumps although it wasn't cold at the time.

Shortly after this disturbing incident, Belinda became quite ill, partly from exhaustion, and had to take a week off from her work. She considers the two events could be connected.

In the bar area and the adjoining dining rooms, on several occasions footsteps have been heard crossing the rooms, with a heavy and deliberate tread. A man has been seen here dressed in a soldier's uniform, and looking out of place. The flat on the first floor is currently used by the manageress. It is reputedly haunted by a former landlady, named Ethel, who hanged herself on the premises. In her own small way, she seems never to have left. Ethel has been seen by various customers and staff over the years since her death, both in the bar and in Belinda's flat. Belinda told me that for some reason the ghost continually moves toiletries, soaps, deodorants and so on from the bathroom to the kitchen.

One male visitor had a particularly vivid experience of seeing Ethel in the kitchen of the flat. It was during the tenancy of the previous manageress. He saw a kindly, grey-haired, elderly woman in the kitchen and presumed it to be his friend's mother. He handed the woman two dirty dishes, which she obligingly placed in the sink. He was shocked to find out later that he had seen a ghost, as no such woman was staying in the flat at the time; also, she clearly fitted Ethel's description.

Immediately above on the second floor and reached by a steep staircase is barmaid Andrea's flat. It consists of several adjoining attic rooms, with wonderful countryside views from the dormer windows and dark-stained oak beams. This flat is haunted too, but it doesn't appear to bother cheerful Andrea. She told me she is fairly happy to live with her invisible flatmate. In the corner of the lounge a man once hanged himself from one of the beams. The room is often strangely cold and Andrea told me that any electrical equipment placed in that corner of the room always malfunctions. Her stereo system and radio had been subject to a lot of interference.

In the far room, now used as a bedroom, there is ghostly activity thought to be caused by a little girl, Anna, who lived at the pub probably in the last century. One morning, Andrea was woken up by scrabbling and banging noises coming from the corner built-in cupboard. Initially she thought it might be rats, but on investigation no evidence of vermin was found. On another occasion, she came into the kitchen to find all of the teaspoons stacked up together as a sort of sculpture.

At the rear of the pub, on land now used as the children's playground (it was donated to the children of Ecton by the pub) is a gallows tree. It is situated by some crossroads, which are said by locals to be haunted by a nun. She is said to attempt to stop anyone on horseback, or, much rarer these days, any travellers in a horse-drawn carriage. This occurs every 31 October, Halloween. It has become something of a local legend. Barmaid Andrea told me that every year without fail on Halloween night the pub quickly empties after closing time and the customers make their rowdy way to the spot on the road where the nun is supposed to appear.

When I visited the World's End for the first time, at the beginning of June 1998, I was particularly struck by the fact that certain areas of the building were unnaturally cold. These were the areas reputed to be haunted, or where inexplicable things had happened.

The incident in the cellar reminded me of the story of the cellar in York and the Roman soldiers seen there by a workman, Harry Martindale, in 1953. He was just 18 years old at the time and working as a plumber, installing some central heating in the Treasurer's house in York. As he proceeded to knock a hole through the ceiling, a Roman soldier suddenly stepped out of the wall. He did not realize it at the time, but his ladder was placed on the former route of the old Roman road.

The soldier was followed by about 20 other soldiers and horses, and a sound rather like a bugle. Just as the delivery man at the World's End saw the figure only from the knees upwards, so Mr Martindale saw these men and horses clearly above knee level, but nothing below. The road had only been excavated from the central part of the cellar. The original level of the road in the time of the Romans was some 45 cm (18 in) lower, which explained why they appeared as they did. The only other sound the plumber heard was a murmuring, rather than any specific speech. He was able to see their uniforms clearly and give a detailed description later on.

This has become a classic and much-reported case, typical of the recording type. I find it significant that the young man witnessed this after banging on the ceiling to make a hole for the heating pipes. Perhaps his heavy banging shook the walls of the building and the vibration travelled down to the cellar floor, where it released the images and sounds stored there for possibly 1,500 years.

Going back to our original story, the World's End pub has an extremely benign and friendly atmosphere despite its tragic and often colourful history (it is the site of two hangings and a shooting). I was later able to conduct an all-night ghost investigation there (see Case 28).

CASE 28 | THE GHOSTWATCH AT ECTON

IN LATE June, 1998, I and eight others met up at the World's End public house for an all-night ghostwatch. Dennis Moyses had travelled from Peterborough to attend. My sister Kate, mediums Paul and Sue Hopgood, Belinda Blackmore the pub manageress, and three other members of staff also attended. To be fair, none of us expected too much to happen, and indeed the evening was not all that eventful. However, a few strange incidents did occur and on balance I felt it to have been worth all the effort.

We eventually emptied the pub of customers and numerous staff hangers-on who were all desperate to attend (there had been a small write-up in the local *Chronicle and Echo* newspaper a few days earlier). I was very keen to restrict the numbers of investigators, as too many people spoil the atmosphere and it can become undisciplined. I began with a brief run-through of the history of the pub and the three areas of it that we were to study that night. The first was the cellar, the second the children's play area and the adjacent stairs, and the third the bar. I felt that these areas would prove to be quite active, or at least had the potential to be. We then divided into three groups of three.

Dennis, barmaid Mandy and I were in group A; Kate, Belinda and a young girl member of staff were in group B; and Paul, Sue and a young lad called David were in group C. I proposed that we each spend an hour in every location, and at the termination of each stint Dennis would enthusiastically blow his whistle to signal the changeover. At each changeover we would all meet up in the bar to swap notes before the next stint.

My group spent the first hour in the cellar. We took stools down there with us, and to aid concentration and create the right atmosphere we sat mainly in the dark. Dennis had a torch which he was to use only if needed. It was naturally very cold down in the cellar, and as we sat in the dark listening to the noisy droning of the ice-making machine Dennis felt his face and hand being lightly touched. He said it felt like a fly and when he turned on the torch briefly in the dim beam of light we saw lots of tiny flying insects (Belinda told us later these are called beer flies).

Then Mandy and I heard a sound behind us, like a man coughing and clearing his throat. We all then heard this several times. It appeared to be coming from an area behind us where the wines are stored. I asked Dennis to lend me his torch and went to the back of the cellar. Any illusions of a supernatural cause for the coughing were soon shattered, for the strange noises were all made by the old ice-making machine in the corner (it was quite hard to believe this at first as the 'cough' sounded all too human).

Disappointed, we resumed our seats and extinguished the light. Nothing much else happened except that Mandy felt one of her legs and her foot freeze and become painful. She could think of no rational explanation for this, and the numbness and pain persisted all night. She also saw two tiny pinpricks of light that danced around in the far corner. It did feel very eerie and atmospheric down there and we all felt a presence – of what I'm not quite sure, but in the inky blackness after midnight it felt as if we were being watched. There was the sensation of eyes upon us, aware of us being there. When the hour was up, Dennis blew his whistle so loudly I joked that 'it could wake the dead'.

The ghostwatch at Ecton. Left to right: Paul and Sue Hopgood, the author, and Belinda Blackmore (photograph courtesy of the Chronicle and Echo*).*

For Kate, Belinda and the young girl, who was to look nervous throughout the evening, the stint in the bar area had been quite unnerving. At one point, Belinda's dog had become upset and begun barking at thin air in the corner of the room.

Paul and Sue Hopgood and a white-faced and shaking David came upstairs from the children's play area. David at one point had become quite dizzy and felt a bit 'weird'. They had all felt this area to be quite active, especially the passageway linking the children's soft play area and a small sitting room.

We also discovered that in the far wall of the room there is a door that has been kept locked for over seven years. Belinda told us that the key to the room has been lost but that staff and a number of customers have felt something malevolent to be behind that blue door. Belinda has slid some crystals under the door in an attempt to quiet any negative ghostly activity there. The staff plan to get a carpenter to force open the door to find out what lies behind it once and for all. Personally, when our group spent an hour in these rooms I detected no nasty feelings near to or around this door. As these rooms have very little natural light, being in the basement, I believe this accounts for their dingy and depressing aura. Also, it is quite normal for the human imagination to concoct wonderful scenarios behind the mystery of a long-closed door.

We then swapped shifts. Group C went into the cellar, group A was in the bar, and Group B set up in the play area.

In the bar, we turned off most of the lights and sat in semi-darkness. Dennis entertained us with stories of some of his many ghostwatches over the years. Suddenly, we all heard the faint sound of clicking from near the bar. This occurred several times, and I likened it to the sound of someone striking a match. The only problem was that we three were the only people in the room and none of us was making the noise. After hearing the sound a few times, we were left baffled as to its cause. Nothing else of note occurred, and at 2.30am Dennis blew the whistle again and we all swapped notes.

Group C had felt absolutely nothing during their stint in the cellar, although amusingly they had all been attacked by the annoying beer flies. Group B had felt a little uneasy in the basement rooms. Kate reported sporadically smelling an odour resembling that of methylated spirits (however, I suppose a chemical could have been spilt on the carpet down there). They had also felt a watchful presence, coming from the far left-hand corner, which seemed far from friendly.

Belinda told me that this area had been damaged by flooding at the pub, which occurred a couple of days after my initial visit. It had caused extensive damage and nuisance, but the plumber had been unable to find the cause, as there were no leaking pipes. The worst damage, however, had been in the ladies' toilets. Indeed that area had been closed off for several days, as the smell had been quite sickening.

We were to find this out for ourselves when Mandy, Sue and I visited the toilets during the evening's proceedings. We noticed a disgusting smell there, quite unlike the usual musty smells associated with damp old buildings. The stench reminded me of rotten flesh or spoiled meat.

For our final hour's stint, Group A was in the basement play area, Group B in the cellar and Group C in the bar. Mandy, Dennis and I were a little disappointed when we sensed nothing at all in our final area. We sat in the dark silently at first and heard and saw nothing of a paranormal nature. To relieve the boredom, we began chatting on subjects as diverse as the French revolution, the Bermuda Triangle, and the enigmas posed by UFOs. Soon the hour had slipped by, and we made our weary way upstairs.

None of the groups had much to report; however, the tape-recorder that I had left running in the empty dining room (in the hope of catching any unusual sounds) had been tampered with in our absence. The pause button had been pressed.

To finish off the evening, we all had a drink and all those assembled professed to have enjoyed the evening. Most of them had never attended a ghostwatch before and I was glad that they hadn't considered it to have been a waste of time. We all made our separate ways home as the early morning light appeared.

Paul and Sue Hopgood asked Belinda to keep in touch if she had any more trouble of a supernatural nature at the pub. It was quite an interesting evening, although by the last hour I felt tired. Unfortunately, none of us intrepid ghost-hunters saw any ghosts; but we all had at least strongly felt the presence of 'something'. I plan to conduct another such vigil there very soon, this time with fewer participants.

SNIPPETS OF THE PAST

CAN WE always believe all that we see? Just because we see something does not mean that it is real and still exists. Remnants of the past are all around us in the buildings in which we live, and in the landscape. The past is inescapable. Such is also the case with ghosts, some of which bear dramatic testimony to this past.

Most of us can quickly sense an atmosphere when we first walk into a building. Sceptics might argue that it is just the decor, condition or age of the building that we are picking up on. I believe there is more to it than that, but that the process is a very subtle one. Some people are more able to do this than others. Think, for example, of the common situation of entering a room shortly after two people have been arguing in it. Most of us would instinctively pick up on this and comment later, 'You could have cut the atmosphere with a knife.' We have all done it, and it goes to prove that we do instinctively know things.

This ability may stem from our ancestry as apes. Unable to use complex language, our instincts would have been vital, especially the ability to sense disagreement and imminent fighting. It's easy to see how this would have helped to protect our distant ancestors. They could have either tried to placate those concerned or hidden until a time of safety.

Perhaps a lot of unhappiness and misfortune would and could be avoided if we all obeyed the feelings given to us by 'hunches'. These could simply be nothing more than a primitive early-warning system, there for a good reason, and consisting of skills that are worth understanding and developing. Although we are now considered the 'highest' of animals, our skills in this area now seem to be the lowest.

CASE 29 | OF DREAMS AND HORSES

I T IS funny how unusual happenings in people's lives can sometimes have coincidental links that bind the experiences together. This was to be the case with Sarah Clift from Grimsby. In 1996 she was visiting her boyfriend in Sleaford, Lincolnshire. It was the weekend, and the couple went for a quiet drink in a local pub. It is a very old establishment situated on the main road through the town. Sarah's boyfriend was at the bar buying her a drink, when she glanced towards the end of the bar. Sarah saw a very short, middle-aged man in an old-fashioned shirt staring straight at her. Within the fraction of a second that it took her to blink, the man had gone.

Shocked, Sarah got up and looked around the corner near where the exit was, but the figure was nowhere to be seen. This seemed very odd, as she knew he could not have walked out of the bar and out of sight in such a short time, literally in the blinking of an eye. Sarah's friends asked her what was wrong, as she had gone very white and was shaking. She lightheartedly told them she had just seen a ghost.

Sarah told me that she is now unsure as to whether she saw a ghost or a glimpse of history – a replay of the past, something akin to a tape-recording. The only disconcerting thing about the experience was how the man had stared directly into her eyes.

When Sarah returned to work on the following Monday, she told a colleague about her experience. The friend was not at all surprised, however, as she could describe the man in the pub in great detail. Apparently the workmate's mother, who had an interest in spirits, had a pamphlet regarding the ghosts of Lincolnshire. The pub in question had a well-known ghost of a man who had been trampled to death in an earlier century by horses outside the pub. The road in front of the pub was a route to the cattle market in the town and had always been busy with the traffic of horses and cattle in previous times.

A month after the pub ghost sighting, Sarah went to the seaside town of Whitby for the weekend. She stayed in an old coaching inn that had recently re-opened after extensive refurbishment. It was a beautiful old building and still retained much of its character. Her room opened out onto the hallway, and opposite the room were some windows that overlooked an alleyway running alongside the inn.

On her first night there, Sarah had a very vivid dream that a horse was running up and down the hallway outside her room. Because the dream was so unusual, Sarah mentioned it to the owner of the inn while in conversation at breakfast. He told her that it was odd, as a man had been trampled to death by a horse in the alleyway next to the inn.

Sarah was left wondering what the odds were, in such a short space of time, of somebody visiting two old pubs that had stories associated with them of death by stampeding horses. She also wondered how she had managed to pick up on these events and somehow sense them centuries afterwards.

This case illustrates the beauty of coincidence. The universe appears to thrive on it.

CASE 30 THE OLD WOMAN IN THE HALLWAY

DAWN'S HOME is situated opposite Abington Park in Northampton, and is an imposing house built in 1900. Its front garden was bursting with yellow and purple spring flowers at the time of my visit. Interestingly, the house overlooks a folly in the park that stands on the site where the last witches in the town were burned in the Middle Ages – a time when superstition often overruled common sense and branding an unfortunate scapegoat as a witch was often seen as a cure for all unexplained phenomena.

As you enter the house, you walk into a wide hallway with a beautiful, carved-oak staircase. This hallway was to prove significant when the family related their story to me later on. Dawn and her husband Michael told me that they had lived in the house for years and loved it because of its friendly atmosphere. Shortly after moving in, the couple and their two daughters Charlie and Louise, now teenagers, noticed many strange incidents. A shadowy, floating, grey figure has been seen on the stairs by Michael, and also by a family friend, on two separate occasions. One of the first-floor bedrooms is always unnaturally cold, even in summer; this is where Charlie sleeps. It is a pretty room, decorated in pink, with a bed piled high with teddy bears. One day Charlie was petrified to see the brass keyhole cover spin around on its own.

The kitchen has also been the scene of a lot of disruptive activity in the house. On one wall is a dresser, the sort that is fitted into a wall recess. One day the couple were amazed to see the dresser door open all on its own and a cookbook fall out onto the floor. Later on, a small clock hanging from one of the dresser hooks was found smashed, as was a lightbulb, with its screw attachment still in the socket. Other phenomena experienced by the family include a child's music box playing by itself, and drops of water plopping on Michael while he was in the bath.

Because of this catalogue of unexplained incidents over the years, the couple looked into the history of the house and discovered some interesting facts, facts which I believe may have a direct bearing on the case. The house has only ever had two previous owners. The first was a woman who lived there with her maid for around 60 years. Apparently, when she became old and infirm, the woman locked up all the doors to the downstairs rooms and lived entirely in the hallway, using the fireplace there for heating.

Perhaps in some way the old woman's spirit has never left, and it is she who is haunting the place. From time to time, to make her presence felt, she moves things, and even appears in shadowy form on the stairs. Maybe her presence will gradually dissipate like perfume sprayed into the air – the droplets of fragrance linger for a time, then slowly disappear.

The people concerned in this case are all quite used to the phenomenon in their house and indeed love the place so much they would hate to move away. I cannot blame them, as I found the atmosphere pleasant and calm, and the house had obviously had a lot of time, care and money lavished on it over the years.

CASE 31 | A GRANDMOTHER'S LOVE

FROM THE age of three, Robert Hayden from Merseyside was brought up by his grandparents. Consequently, he was very close to them. Some years later, when his grandmother died, he found it very hard to get used to her not being around any more. Robert and his grandfather often visited the cemetery together to lay flowers on her grave, and then the two would walk sadly home.

Not long after his grandmother's death, Robert's grandfather had to visit the grave alone as Robert was ill with pleurisy and asleep in the arm-chair. Robert awoke to see his grandmother sitting opposite him in the room; she looked entirely normal in every way, as in life, and smiled at her grandson fondly, which gave him tremendous comfort. He laughed later when recalling the incident, as there was his poor grandfather visiting his wife's grave with flowers, when she was back at home all the time.

When his grandfather returned, Robert told him about the incident, but was given a ticking off and told it was due to delirium from the pleurisy. This was not the case, however, as Robert saw further glimpses of his grandmother around the house in the months that followed. He found this phenomenon somewhat confusing, and confided in one of his schoolteachers. She listened kindly and advised him not to talk to anyone else about it, as they perhaps would not understand.

After leaving school, Robert got a job that necessitated him getting up at 6am. He found it very difficult to do so every morning, and on several occasions he told me that his alarm had failed to go off. It did not matter, though, as he heard his grandmother call him from the bottom of the stairs urging him to wake up. Apparently, she had always done this when she was alive, to get him up in time for school. It would seem that Robert's grandmother haunted him because she still wanted to love and care for her grandson, even after death.

The experience has been nothing but positive for Robert. This is often the case when the bereaved are comforted in such a tangible way by their loved ones.

CASE 32 | THE HANGED MAN

THE NEXT case was related to me by Mark, an actor living in the Northamptonshire village of Moulton. Mark has appeared in many films in his career, including *Return of the Jedi*, one of the *Star Wars* trilogy, and *Labyrinth*. He was also star of many a pantomime over the years in various theatres. In all that time, he had never encountered anything remotely inexplicable, until his stint at a theatre in Maidstone, Kent, in the late 1980s. The theatre is called the Hazlett and is very small;

its capacity at most is only 200–300 people. Although it is fairly old, Mark did not really expect the place to be haunted, although it was reputed to be.

An incident occurred during an evening performance of the popular show *Snow White and the Seven Dwarves*. The show was in mid-season and all the actors had settled in to a routine. Mark told me that it is usual at such a time, well into the run of a show, for all the actors to have relaxed into their roles, and much ad-libbing and general fun is to be had by all. They were approaching the end of Scene 2, and all the actors were on stage. Mark and his friend Peter were standing slightly to the front of the others, on stage right. It was the scene where the dwarves find Snow White in their cottage. The curtain went down to the strains of the song 'Whistle While You Work'.

The two actors were standing directly next to the theatre wings, which at the time were empty. The stage curtain was halfway down and all the actors had taken a bow, when they heard and felt footsteps behind them. Peter felt someone brush him on their way past. The noise of the footsteps was heard by the pair, even above the frenzied clapping of the audience, which Mark said was very loud that evening as the cast had all given a good performance.

They looked behind them and to their surprise saw no-one. They had at first assumed the footsteps to be those of one of the stage hands coming out too soon before the curtain had fully descended. As they left the stage, Mark commented to Peter how cold it had become on stage. As he patted his friend Peter on the back, he recoiled in horror: the whole of Peter's back was bitterly cold. Mark told me it felt as if he was touching ice. The strange thing was that the actor's clothing at the front was of a normal temperature. The two actors realized that they had had a brush with something out of the ordinary.

Talking to the other actors later, after a few stiff drinks, Mark and Peter were disbelieved at first, as none of the others had seen or heard anything untoward. However, discussions about the incident with a woman who knew about the theatre's history uncovered a very curious and tragic story. It was rumoured that, decades earlier, one of the stage hands had accidentally been hanged on one of the ropes attached to the stage curtain. The chap was young, and somehow he had become entangled in the ropes. This had been the only death connected to the 100-year-old theatre, and Mark still wonders if this was the man who walked behind them that night on the stage. He feels that he will never be able to forget this event.

Theatres often have a history of ghostly activity and superstition. Actors are, after all, very superstitious. Perhaps this is largely psychological; their very profession is often precarious, to say the least. This is maybe why they are at pains to encourage good luck and avoid bad luck in their many superstitions. For example, it is considered very bad luck to speak the name of Shakespeare's play *Macbeth* – instead, it is referred to as 'The Scottish Play'.

CASE 33 | THE CRYING GIRL

HELEN WHITEHEAD, from Ealing in London, was only 13 when she had her experience of seeing a ghost. She was staying at a friend's house, which dated back to the early Victorian era. Helen and her friend were sharing a double bed in the spare room when she became aware during the night of a sniffing and snivelling noise coming from the corner of the bedroom. Helen thought at first that it was her friend's younger sister who had a bad cold, and when her eyes became used to the dark she saw the silhouette of a young girl in the corner of the room. However, the small girl was not anyone that Helen knew, and, becoming afraid, she shook her friend to wake her. The girls switched on the light, but there was nobody in the corner, and they both became very frightened indeed.

After that, sleep was impossible. In the morning, Helen's friend told one of her relatives, who had lived in the house for many years, of the previous night's scare. Others who had stayed had also told the woman about the apparition of a crying girl, who it was believed had lived in the house in Victorian times.

On the next evening the two girls tried to sleep in the spare room again, but halfway through the night they became too afraid and had to sleep in another room. Since then, Helen tells me that her friend's younger sister has moved into the 'haunted room' but has not seen or heard any trace of the crying girl. Maybe the ghostly girl can only make her presence felt when somebody with a sensitive disposition sleeps in that room; or perhaps she is a type of recording from the past, only re-activated at certain times.

This case could well be a so-called 'anniversary ghost', that some-how chooses the day and date for its return. Such hauntings follow a cyclical pattern and are far from being rare.

Crying ghosts from all parts of the British Isles have been written about for centuries. I suppose the Irish equivalent would be the wailing banshee – a restless spirit whose crying is a portent of imminent death or misfortune to the family who hear her wails.

CASE 34 THE PHANTOM CAR

SIMON HAS had many brushes with the paranormal over the years, beginning in the late 1960s. He describes himself as very sensitive to atmospheres and is probably a natural 'medium'.

Simon's first odd incident occurred in 1967; he arrived home after an evening out with friends and settled down into bed. It was then that he felt a presence outside the bedroom window. It felt most unfriendly, and puzzled by this the young man looked outside. Nothing was to be seen, and so he just shrugged it off.

The second time, a few weeks later, Simon once again felt a nasty presence outside the window. He raced to the window and looked out. Below, near the pavement, was an extremely bright light, and he felt an atmosphere of utter malevolence. Simon quickly went downstairs and opened the front door, but the mysterious light had gone.

Simon got married, some years after this, to Beryl, and they had a daughter they named Abigail. When she was about nine years old the family had a day out in the Cotswolds at a wildlife park. They were par-ticularly interested in visiting the reptiles, and, on the way to see some fruitbats housed next to these, they had to walk through the old court-yard. This was next to the country house in the grounds of which the wildlife park is sited. The buildings here are part of an old stable block.

It was a hot summer's day and the site was full of visitors. Abigail suddenly pushed her parents out of the way and screamed that a big black car had almost hit them all. Simon and Beryl were shaken and angry, as no-one had seen or heard any car. The courtyard was full of peo-ple; no vehicles were anywhere to be seen.

Later, during a conversation with the keeper at the reptile house, Simon was told that the wildlife park had been taken over by the government during the Second World War and used by the American military. On the way home in the car, Abigail was still adamant about what she had seen, and the couple were left wondering if somehow their daughter had seen a ghostly recorded image of the past. After all, during the war the American military has used large black cars such as the one described by their little girl 40 years later. Such vehicles are not in general use today.

The family are unsure as to why they were the only ones who saw the phantom car that day, and whether the vehicle could have actually run them over or caused them any real physical harm if they had remained in its path. I believe this to be extremely unlikely, as this incident has all the hallmarks of a recording-type event and nothing more. As such, it is no more real and three-dimensional than a hologram, although disturbing nevertheless.

CASE 35 STONEMASONS' TALES

THESE TWO stories were related to me by Mr H.M. Youd, after being told to him by two of his work colleagues. Mr Youd spoke of his work experiences as a stonemason, and how over many years he had repaired and restored old colleges and churches. He was very much responsible for looking after part of the historic heritage of Great Britain. The first story related to Mr Youd came from a close friend whom I shall call Eric. It occurred during the Second World War when Eric was a boy.

One clear moonlit night, Eric and a few friends set out with the intention of poaching a few unwitting pheasants; this was pretty much a necessity during the war years owing to the lack of fresh meat. The boys could clearly see the resting forms of the pheasants in the trees from where they had positioned themselves along the road which ran from Walborough village out into the Oxfordshire countryside. As the boys stood scanning the view of the treetops, they heard the chatter of many voices approaching them. On hearing the voices the boys ducked into the hedgerow. As they watched, they could clearly make out the silhouettes of perhaps 30 people passing by in the cold night.

The group was very loud and boisterous and could still be heard clearly even when they had passed over a slight hill further down the road where they walked out of sight. The curious boys decided to follow the unusual and noisy night-time party of adults in case they were missing out on some fun. As they reached the rise in the road, they were suddenly greeted with a wall of silence; the road ahead was entirely empty. Bewildered, the boys looked around, surprised that the noisy group had simply vanished – there was nowhere that they could have hidden. The frightened boys ran home quickly with all thoughts of poaching entirely forgotten.

Thirty years later, Eric was driving along one dark evening with his wife. Their journey took them along a road that joined the villages of Walborough and Dorchester-on-Thames. Suddenly Eric's wife exclaimed, 'Who are they?' Eric automatically slowed the vehicle as the car's headlights illuminated something very strange. A group of people was moving along the left-hand side of the road towards Eric's car. They were walking in a somewhat military style, in two columns, with the inner column of walkers appearing much shorter in height than the outer column, and they were clearly holding hands. The people in the procession were all dressed in monks' habits. Although Eric and his wife tried, they were not able to see a single face beneath the raised hoods: the entire group of over 20 individuals was faceless.

When they first sighted the group, the couple assumed them to be party-goers, as it was near to Halloween. However, the couple felt that they might have witnessed something of a supernatural origin, owing to the bizarre lack of facial features. Eric then remembered the incident of the vanishing revellers on the same stretch of road 30 years earlier.

The area around Walborough, Dorchester and Shillingford has a rich history; there is an abundance of earthworks, and locals claim that the Dorchester–Walborough road runs alongside the site of a now-demolished medieval hamlet that was totally wiped out by the Black Death. This was not uncommon – the Black Death was known to have decimated a small hamlet outside the Northamptonshire village of Harpole; the only memory of the hamlet, called Glassthorpe, is a lane named after it in the village of Harpole, and a few building stones scattered in the surrounding fields.

The two roadside incidents related in this case could quite easily be some type of recording of a past event.

The second story involves another colleague of Mr Youd, whom I shall call Brian. In the early 1970s, Brian and several workmates were called upon to go to Dorchester Abbey in Dorset to assist with renovation work taking place there. They were curious at first because, although their company had originally put in a tender, another a company from Bristol had started the work. Dorchester Abbey is a beautiful example of early English medieval architecture, and is much noted for the intricate tracery of the windows. Dorchester as a town has been an important religious site since early Anglo-Saxon times. When Brian and his workmates arrived on site at the Abbey, the scene was somewhat reminiscent of the *Marie Celeste*, in that tools lay scattered and abandoned all around the work site, and buckets of stone-dust putty had been left to harden. A puzzled Brian approached the resident vicar, who explained exactly what had taken place.

The three original craftsmen had for some reason been working through the night, presumably to catch up on lost time. One night they were having a tea break, when suddenly the heavy wooden pews started to rock violently as if moved by some unseen force. They watched with a mixture of amazement and fear, and after a number of seconds everything simply stopped dead. However, the display was not over: a pew nearest to the men suddenly shot forward until it stopped a mere foot from them. Terrified, they fled from the abbey, and drove rapidly and without stopping until they reached the safety of Bristol.

Brian and his colleagues fared much better at the haunted abbey, with none of the team experiencing any unusual happenings; however, they did refuse to work after dark.

CASE
36 FRANK

NANCY'S EXPERIENCE was to help her get over the sudden death of her husband and has given her comfort on remembering it since. Nancy is the wife of the famous artist, the late Frank Bellamy. He was well known for his contributions in the *Eagle* comic books and also for drawing the series of 'Garth' cartoons for the *Daily Mirror*. His paintings of the Masai tribe of Africa are especially splendid.

The couple lived in the village of Geddington, just outside Kettering. In the late 1970s, Nancy had just returned from a short holiday with her sister. She was shocked by the appearance of Frank on her return, as he looked so tired and drawn. Frank died suddenly that night, somewhat prematurely at the age of 59. Nancy's experience happened two or three days after the funeral of her much-loved husband.

Because of her distress, the doctor had given the widow some tablets to help her sleep. She was just drifting off, when she heard a voice in the hall of the bungalow calling 'Nancy, Nancy', over and over again. Opening her eyes, Nancy saw her husband standing in the bedroom at the side of her bed; he was so near that if she had reached out she could have touched him.

He looked so relaxed, young and happy, as if the years had rolled away. Frank's hands were crossed on his chest and, as in life, he was wearing his favourite colour green (it had been a family joke that the artist had always chosen green for his clothes). Within seconds he had gone and Nancy fell asleep, overwhelmed by a feeling of peace and happiness. Some time later, when Nancy told her sister of the experience, her sister said that Frank had visited her too.

The last few years have not been easy for Nancy Bellamy, but she told me that without her close encounter with the spirit of her dead husband the loss would have been much harder to bear. At least now she is more certain of the survival of the human spirit after death. Frank's pictures continue to be enjoyed by today's youngsters, as many of his cartoons of Gerry Anderson's *Thunderbirds* series have recently been republished. His fame lives on and will do so as long as a new generation of children is able to enjoy his splendid cartoons and vision.

CASE 37 | THE PIPESMOKER

SHEILA B, who is a former neighbour of mine from Bugbrooke, Northamptonshire, told me of a very curious incident. It happened to a close relative of hers, in the nearby village of Harpole (see also Case 35), many years ago, but is interesting as it features both an apparent 'time-slip' and the sighting of an apparition.

Sheila's family lived at Carr House, a large sandstone building which stands on a high grassy bank. A street in the village is named after the house – this is Carr's Way. Originally the building had a lot of land situated around the back, which was sold off for new houses as the village expanded.

One day, Sheila's grandfather came into the house. As he entered through the back door, he suddenly realized that the room was different in some way. There, sitting cosily by a fireplace, was an elderly gentleman, someone that he didn't recognize, smoking a pipe. (At that time in Carr House no such fireplace existed.) The shock of the scene before him was such that it caused him to faint to the floor, where his wife soon found him, out cold.

When he came round, the room was completely back to normal. He told his family about his 'vision', but he was still a little in shock and did not really understand what had occurred. Later on, the family discovered that there had indeed been a fireplace in the exact spot where the grandfather had seen it. This gave some credence to his story, as none of them had known prior to his experience that this fireplace had existed. This led

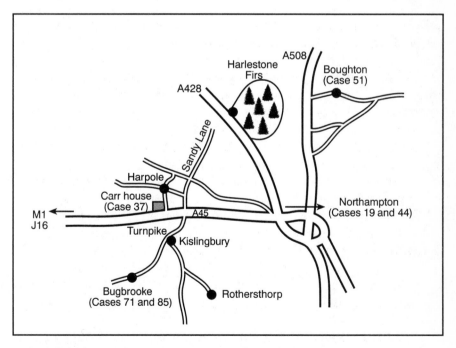

A few of the haunted Northamptonshire villages featured in this book.

them to believe that perhaps he had glimpsed a brief moment from the old house's past. What caused this to happen on that particular day was, naturally, a mystery.

It is intriguing to consider what might have happened if the grandfather in this story had not fainted but tried to engage the pipesmoker in conversation, or even gone on to explore further rooms in the house. Would they all have been a part of the same era as the one he accidently stepped into that day? Or was the 'recording' restricted entirely to that one small room at the back of the house?

This incident is unusual, in that following reports from someone claiming to have experienced a time-slip, there is often no evidence found to back up and lend credence to the story.

CASE 38 IN THE WOODS

ON ST PATRICK'S Day in 1997, Mrs J. Sharpe and her husband were out walking with their dogs in Salcey Forest, Northamptonshire. As they walked along the main track through the forest, they came to a junction in the road, giving a choice of three possible routes ahead. It was here that they saw a man, about 2 m (6 ft) tall and dressed in the unmistakable attire of a cavalier.

The man had shoulder-length hair, a red shirt, and a thick leather belt with a large, polished, metal buckle. He wore long leather boots and sported a very long and thin moustache. As they approached him, the couple assumed the man either to be in fancy dress or to be part of a historical group that re-enacts historic scenes and battles for the public.

Mr Sharpe said hello to the man as they passed, but received no reply. Thinking the man to be ignorant, deaf or just rude, the couple gave each other a puzzled look before turning round to catch another glimpse of the strangely clad man who looked so out of place in the quiet of the forest. As they turned around, only seconds after speaking to him, they were amazed to find that the cavalier had vanished. They just couldn't understand it. Unless the man had run very quickly and was hidden behind a tree or crouched low in the undergrowth, and they hadn't heard his running footsteps, there was nowhere for him to have gone. All the three branches of the road were empty. If he had continued along one of these routes, he would inevitably have been visible. It was at this moment that the Sharpes jointly considered aloud that they had just seen a ghost, one who had been totally unaware of their presence, hence his silence when Mr Sharpe spoke.

There have been other sightings and strange phenomena reported to me associated with Salcey Forest. One was an alleged sighting of a UFO hovering over the trees, spotted by two men travelling past in their car. There are also rumours of witchcraft ceremonies being carried out in the depths of the forest at night.

Sightings of cavaliers are common, and have been reported many times from all over Great Britain. I read of a recent case in the *Fortean Times* where one was spotted by some girls on the way to a disco. Most of these apparitions sound to me as though they fit very well into the recording-type category, especially as they seem so unaware of those around them in the twentieth century. Their distinctive dress means they are easily noticed, looking so incongruous in their surroundings.

The only other possibility is that this man was indeed in fancy dress that day in the forest, and, needing to relieve himself, quickly ran into the cover of the trees.

CASE 39 COLD AND HOT

ALTHOUGH SHE has long since moved away, Elaine C used to live in a small cottage near to a park in Northamptonshire. The cottage was very picturesque, with tiny leaded windows and a heavy, old, oak front door complete with the original iron furnishings. The gardens in front were crammed with a profusion of colour all year round, consisting mainly of foxgloves, roses and hollyhocks. The cottage felt welcoming and cosy inside, except that on occasion Elaine could sense a slight change in atmosphere. When this happened, the corner of the lounge became very cold and her small dog Troy would stand in the corner of the room barking, almost as if there were an intruder standing there.

The stairs were in two parts with a right-angled turn. On the first area of landing, Elaine kept a narrow mahogany bookcase. Being an avid reader, she had books all over the house. Often when she went up the stairs, on this landing she would smell the scent of lavender very strongly. She told me that it was extremely pungent, and as she very much dislikes lavender she couldn't understand its origin. She had no lavender in her garden, nor did any of her immediate neighbours. Also she had never used any soaps, lotions or furniture polish containing this aroma that could perhaps have accounted for it. On most days the smell was absent, but at least once or twice a month it would return, as strong as ever.

Visitors had also commented on this, so she knew it was not her imagination. Friends just presumed her to be using an incense-burner, or to have spilt some perfume onto the carpet of the landing.

One July in the late 1980s, Elaine was having a party for a few friends. The weather all day had been hot and muggy as if a storm were brewing. Elaine has always been badly affected by changes in the weather and finds (as indeed I do myself) that either a rise or fall in air pressure can bring on a bad headache and change in mood. Elaine had opened up all of the windows in her house to let in some air.

One of her friends, whom I shall call Lesley, went upstairs to visit the bathroom. A few minutes later the party-goers downstairs heard screams and then the thud of someone falling downstairs. Elaine and her friend Bob rushed to see what had happened and found Lesley collapsed on the landing.

Suspecting that she was perhaps a bit drunk, as they had all been drinking quite a bit, they helped her slowly downstairs, and someone busily made her a black coffee. They were worried to see that Lesley was shivering, and despite the heat felt cold to the touch. When she had eventually calmed down enough to speak coherently, Lesley told the others exactly what had happened.

On her way up to the bathroom she had been assailed by the pungent smell of lavender. She described it as being as if you had buried your head in a heavily flowering lavender bush during the height of summer and took in a deep breath. It felt heady and overpowering to her in a way, but she liked the scent, which reminded her of her late grandmother who had always worn it.

After finishing in the bathroom, she was almost halfway down the stairs when she saw a small girl standing in front of the bookcase. Lesley, with shock, realized that this little girl must be a ghost, as she could see all the books in the bookcase through her, a bit like viewing something through grubby, grey, net curtains.

The girl was dressed in what amounted to rags. They looked very old, dirty and worn, much too big to fit her properly. Around her shoulders was a little shawl. The face of the girl was sad, pale and thin, with deep grey shadows under her eyes. Lesley became almost transfixed, staring at the ghost. The last thing that she remembers before realization hit was reading the title of a book through the girl's semi-transparent grey form. It was *The Carpetbaggers* by Harold Robbins. She heard herself scream and then found that she had fallen and was surrounded by her concerned friends. No-one else present in the house that evening saw the little ghost. Nor indeed did Elaine during the rest of her time spent living in the cottage.

Lesley has never forgotten her encounter. The sheer overwhelming sadness and poverty of this ragged child had made a deep and lasting impression on her. She believes that the girl is somehow connected to the mysterious smell of lavender and the cold spot in the corner of the lounge. Perhaps she once lived there and is now unable to leave.

CASE 40 THE HAUNTED ROAD

I WAS BORN and brought up in Northamptonshire and it remains one of my favourite locations. The countryside is green and the hills gently undulate. In this piece of middle England, history has left its mark in the numerous old sandstone dwellings, castles, walls and churches.

For the ghost-hunter, my home county provides rich pickings. Perhaps this very abundance of ghostly legends fuelled my interest in this subject from a young age. I also have my father to thank, for his story-telling, especially about the ghosts in and around Northampton, always kept me captivated. Sometimes he would take me in the car to haunted locations. Sadly we never witnessed any spectral activity, but it didn't matter too much. I was the only one who had this interest; my sisters found it all a bit dull.

My favourite location and story (I have no idea as to the verifiable truth of it) was of the haunted road at Upton. It is now a layby, since the A45 road was built to bypass it. Apparently, this stretch of road was so badly haunted that anyone journeying along it at night found the road to be almost impassable. Horses would bolt here or rear up and refuse to go any further. These animals are renowned for being sensitive to atmospheres and are usually terrified of haunted locations. Many was the time when we were driving home that I would make my father turn onto this short stretch of road in the hope of seeing something of the ghostly variety. Of course we never did.

This particular stretch of road is also an accident blackspot, which is so often the case. It could just be coincidence or some kind of negative force that makes accidents more likely. I know of locations of so-called 'phantom' roads. These occur when a length of the roadway has been slightly changed and relocated. Drivers, usually during the hours of darkness, witness the old part of the road up ahead and drive onto it, even though it has long ceased to exist. This has caused deaths and frightening accidents, with witnesses swearing that they have seen and attempted to drive on a road that no longer exists.

Ghosts connected with roads have always held a fascination, whether they be phantom walkers or hitchhikers. Less common are spectral vehicles, ranging from horse-drawn carriages to cars and motorbikes, and even an old London bus. Many British roads follow ley lines and historic pathways.

Maybe it is not so surprising after all that these incidents do occur, considering the number of deaths associated with roads in general.

HARMLESS HAUNTINGS

ERE FOLLOWS a selection of friendly phantoms and fairly harmless hauntings: ghosts that may surprise and maybe cause some disruption, but that mean no ill. They were invariably described almost fondly by those I interviewed.

A case in point is the poltergeist, nicknamed Fred, encountered by Paul and Sue Hopgood. The phenomena experienced by the couple made them both realize their proficiency as mediums and also their talent for design. This talent has flourished; their jewellery and beautiful objects made from all types of unusual stones are very popular and sell well.

This story is but one small example of people turning their brushes with the paranormal into something really positive. Such experiences often cause the experiencer to question radically their often previously very limited view of the world and change their thinking and philosophies accordingly.

I suppose this happened to me, in a way. After my first experience of seeing a ghost, I became much more open-minded to the possibilities that conventional science was wrong in one or two areas. The seemingly impossible levitation of objects, disembodied voices, and visits supposedly from the dead did seem to happen to people – and to very reliable witnesses who couldn't possibly all be mistaken.

The very first ghost I saw was extremely solid-looking, and although I only saw her for a matter of seconds she looked no different than she had done in life (she was a former tenant in the house in which I lived). The incident, because it was so fleeting and no conversation took place between us, left me very puzzled. Sometimes there is no more to the experience of seeing a ghost than this. In such cases, it is easy to try to forget the whole thing and write it off.

This is probably what I would have done if this brief incident had not been followed by many others that lasted considerably longer and had some meaning to them.

41 BILLY

DENNIS MINIHANE wrote to me, telling me of his experiences as a small child living in Cork, Ireland. Because he was so young at the time, his mother had to fill him in on some of the details. His mother and all of his aunts can still remember it all vividly.

It was 1978 and Dennis, who was about two years old, moved with his family into a house that was over a century old. Very soon, Dennis told his mother about his friend Billy; Dennis was apparently the only one who could see him. His mother at first thought it was just a typical case of a lonely child inventing an imaginary friend, a very common occurrence, nothing unusual in that – until the family heard the noises from Dennis' room.

His mother used to put her toddler into his cot for a sleep, and after going downstairs she would hear his toy bike rolling along the carpet upstairs, as if someone was riding it. If she went to check up on him Dennis would still be in his cot; he was unable to get out on his own. Also Dennis would not eat up his dinner unless a place was set for Billy as well.

Relatives sleeping over used to share the room with the toddler, sleeping in the spare bed. They would always comment on the extreme, almost unnatural, coldness of the room. The toys were almost always moved around in the night, and once a two-sided blade left resting in the sink in the room was found in the morning in the child's cot. His sheets were ripped to shreds, but Dennis and his cot were strangely unscathed.

When the time came for the family to move from the house, Dennis' mother, on a whim, went into the child's room and said, 'Billy, if you can't come with us give me a sign'. At that moment a toy leapt from a shelf and fell crashing to the floor.

Dennis told me that he can remember very little of his invisible friend Billy, but the women in his family remember it all well and are still at a loss to explain it. Could it have been the ghost of a child who formerly lived in the house, happy to share the room and toys with another child?

Invisible friends are an almost indispensable part of most of our childhoods, and are often a child's way of overcoming loneliness and boredom. Nevertheless, Dennis believes to this day that Billy was much more than this. Although friendly, there was an element of mischievous menace surrounding his antics. The blade placed in the child's cot could so easily have led to tragedy.

CASE 42 THE SINGING MONK

THE VILLAGE of Guilsborough near Northampton contains many fine historic buildings. Most of them are built of sandstone, which was commonly used in house construction up until modern times when, because it is so expensive, it is seldom used. The High Street, in particular, retains much of the atmosphere of centuries past, as many of the original cottages still remain, unchanged over the passage of time.

Marion W wrote to me about her mother's experience in their cottage in Guilsborough. Although the house only dates back to the 1950s, the front was actually constructed from reclaimed church bricks. Marion W and her mother have lived there for some years now and the incident Marion related to me happened early on, when they first moved into Groom Cottage.

Marion's parents' marriage had broken up and her mother was very upset one night. In her distressed state she was finding it impossible to sleep. Suddenly she was aware of a hooded figure standing at the foot of the bed. She felt an overwhelming feeling of love and compassion which seemed to be emanating from the figure. He sang to her for a time and she fell asleep. Far from being disturbed by the unusual nocturnal visitor, Marion's mother found the experience moving and beautiful.

At first they could not understand why the ghostly figure of a monk would appear in their home. Some delving into the history of the village and the site of Groom Cottage uncovered several interesting facts. There had indeed been a monastery at one time located to the rear of the house.

In addition, the large, grassy banks to the sides of the cottage had been found some years earlier to contain underneath them the remains of several medieval cottages. A number of artifacts had been uncovered by one enthusiastic digger.

One can only speculate as to the reason why the cottages had been buried in this way. Did all the occupants die from the plague, and were these 'unclean' dwellings and their occupants buried *in situ*? Or were they dangerous and falling down, and the crumbling ruins covered over with piles of earth?

Some time later, a friend of Marion's mother slept over in the spare room. He too saw the hooded figure and heard its singing voice. Perhaps this friendly and caring monk still feels drawn to helping those in distress who live near the site of the former monastery, and so he continues to sing the Latin chants as he did centuries before.

In most of the cases I have investigated concerning ghostly monks, I have yet to encounter a malevolent one. Often they bring a sense of peace or comfort to those lucky enough to come into contact with them.

CASE 43 BURIED ALIVE

TWO EDINBURGH students, Drew Watson and David Moran, encountered sinister echoes from the past while sharing a flat at Paisley Close. It was in January 1988 that Drew had his first experience. He was in bed one morning and about to get up, when he heard a voice call 'Drew' in his ear. It was very clear and strong, but he knew it could not be his flatmate David, as he had gone out. Drew leapt out of bed and went to the front door, but it was locked and the flat was empty. He was left with a strange feeling, as he knew it was not his imagination.

The two lads had almost forgotten the disembodied voice incident when, a few months later, David was returning home from Napier College. It was about 6.30pm when he turned off the High Street into Paisley Close. As he walked down the Close towards the flat, he heard heavy footsteps behind him; turning to see who might be following, he was shocked to find no-one there. The sound of the steps continued until they were directly behind him. David rushed into the flat to tell Drew –

he was quite scared by this point. The two became convinced that there were ghosts in the building, and after making some enquiries into the history of the flats at Paisley Close they discovered a moving story.

In the mid-1800s the building where they now lived had collapsed. Like so many buildings at the time used to house the poor, it had been shoddily constructed. People rushed to look for survivors, but it seemed that everyone had perished. A rescuer must have heard something, however, because they discovered a man, John Paisley, who had been buried alive in the rubble. He shouted, 'Heave awa' lads, I'm no' deid yet', and the close is named after him.

Drew and David told me they did not believe in ghosts until the strange events happened; and, as they consider themselves to be pretty level-headed, they do not believe these occurrences to have been figments of either of their imaginations.

The story was reported in the *Edinburgh Evening News* because of local interest in the case. Drew sent me the press cutting concerned. The two lads went public on the incident, despite risking ridicule and the general leg-pulling that often accompanies such a move. This is the reason that I sometimes protect a witness's anonymity by either changing their name or using initials.

CASE 44 THE MONK AND THE MASON

THE GROSVENOR Shopping Centre is situated in the centre of Northampton town (see also Case 19) and overlooks the bustling old market square. Built in the 1980s, the centre has been refurbished in recent years and has an attractive pair of glass lifts and an interior water fountain which is popular with small children shopping with parents, who like to throw pennies into the fountain and make a wish. The shopping mall has had five separate haunting outbreaks reported over the years.

One of these incidents occurred in the small confectioners near one of the exits. My attention had been drawn to the shop after reading about it in the local *Chronicle and Echo* newspaper, and hearing two of the staff talk about it on Radio Northampton. Laura, one of the young girls who worked there, showed me the back storerooms of the shop and the sink area where the workers make tea. It is in this area that most of the activity has taken place.

Lights have turned on and off by themselves; boxes of toffee and chocolates are often found scattered about, even after the shop has been empty overnight; Laura once entered the storeroom and found all of the heavy boxes arranged in a circle. Cold spots are experienced and often an aura of gloom and depression prevails in the upstairs storerooms, which I felt myself when I visited.

A young man working there has been particularly badly affected. One of the girls felt like crying on one occasion, and was pushed by an invisible person. The sound of rattling keys in empty rooms has also been heard. Eventually the staff enlisted the help of a medium to try to understand the phenomena. He told them the spirit was that of the long-deceased keeper of the masonic lodge which was once on the site of the present-day sweet shop. He is now known to all the staff as Charlie.

Another ghost is said to haunt the shopping centre: it is the ghost of a young monk seen carrying a small bush. The rear park of the Grosvenor Centre is built on the grounds of a former monastery, hence the name of the bus station there, which is called Greyfriars. This novice monk has been seen near the escalators at the bus station and is said to walk through the phone boxes as if they do not exist. He has been seen by shoppers and workers alike and, as far as I know, is the only ghost on record that carries a piece of topiary!

CASE 45 | THE COLD ROOM

SHERRY AND Greg live in the Northamptonshire village of Irchester with their three small children. When the family moved into their cottage a few years ago it was in need of total restoration. The house is sited in the High Street of the village and dates back to medieval times when it was used as a meeting hall. It was converted into a house in the late eighteenth century.

Sherry told me that when they moved into the house it was in a bad state, and over the years the couple have done a lot of work on the cottage – restoring the oak beams, opening up an inglenook fireplace in the dining room and restoring the extensive wooden panelling in one of the downstairs rooms. When I visited, the restoration work was almost complete and the house retains much of its original character and charm.

They have three bedrooms upstairs, one of which is now used as a playroom. The couple have had to give up the idea of using this as a child's bedroom as none of the children would settle in there. The room is permanently cold, the reason for which the couple would find out later when Greg had to visit his family for six weeks in his native country of South Africa. Sherry was left running her husband's business and looking after the children.

A conversation one day with her next-door neighbour Karen, during her husband's absence, frightened Sherry, as she was alone at night in the house: Karen asked Sherry if she had encountered the ghostly old lady yet. Apparently, Karen had seen the figure of a woman in Victorian dress enter her bedroom through the wall of Sherry and Greg's old cottage on numerous occasions. Karen said the woman stood by her bed and smiled at her, but her face was cold and oddly menacing, with the sort of smile that does not reach the eyes.

The ghost was perhaps a widow, as she was dressed all in black and was wearing a black lacy hat. This was a common practice in Victorian times: to signify mourning after the loss of her husband, a woman would dress in black for the rest of her life. The room in Sherry's cottage from which the ghost appeared was the children's playroom – the very room in which the children could not sleep and which was permanently chilly despite the central heating.

However, the old lady was not the only person haunting the property. Footsteps are often heard going up and down the oak staircase. It is uncarpeted, so the footsteps are sometimes very loud. The three children would hear the noise and call out for their mother, but she was downstairs all the time.

On one occasion, during a dinner party, a friend of the family was coming out of the bathroom when she saw a strange man descending the stairs. A little taken aback, she told the others at the party about it and they were all puzzled as no-one had even been upstairs.

Despite all the ghostly activity in her home, Sherry told me she loves living there. The house does indeed have a nice atmosphere and a real sense of history about it, but that is perhaps not surprising given its age and interesting past. When I visited Sherry's house recently to ask her permission to take a photograph of the exterior, some building work was taking place there. The kitchen was in the process of being extended.

Pieces of pottery had been found and indeed further on from the cottage's back garden Roman remains have been found. The pottery could even date from such a time.

CASE 46 | AN OPENING OF DOORS

NORTHERN IRELAND has its fair share of ghosts and this next story demonstrates that hauntings do not always last for ever. Jo Morgan wrote to me in 1997 telling me about her family's strange experiences in their house and garden in Newry, County Down.

It all started, as far as they can remember, when her brother was sitting watching football on television. His chair was by the back window of his room when he heard three loud raps on the glass. Suspecting his sister Jo was playing a prank on him and trying to interrupt his television viewing, he pulled back the curtain, but no-one was there. Confused, he came downstairs to the living room where all the family were gathered, and accused Jo of banging on his window. But the whole family knew no-one had left their seats; also the dogs had not barked, which they surely would have done had there been any intruders in the garden.

A month or two later, Jo's father was watching television in the lounge late at night when the door slowly opened and the handle turned. He was afraid, as he knew he was on his own at the time. On another evening, Jo's sister Rose was in her boyfriend's car, parked up in front of the house, when she saw their front door open. She thought it was just her mother being nosy, so she said goodbye to her boyfriend and went inside. When she got into the lounge, both her parents were asleep on the couch. Rose woke them up and asked them who had been so nosy and opened the front door, but they were mystified, as they had both been asleep for ages and had not been near it. They also wondered how she had got in, as the door latch had been down and it was firmly locked.

Over the next six months, the family was plagued by the phenomenon of doors opening and closing by themselves. One morning they even came downstairs to find the front door wide open; they could only be grateful that they lived in a quiet rural area as otherwise they would most surely have been robbed.

Once, when Jo's mother was watching television, she noticed a dark, shadowy, coffin-shaped figure float across the kitchen. On another occasion, Jo's mother saw a little red-haired girl standing in the garden by the fence looking very pale. When Jo's mother went into the kitchen to ask anyone if they knew who the curious red-headed girl was outside, they all went out to look but she had gone. They were left wondering, after the string of events that they had witnessed over the preceding months, if they had just seen not a living child but a ghost of one.

The strange events ceased as suddenly as they had begun. Jo told me that she could not imagine who could have been haunting their home, but it was a very old house before it was renovated in 1988. The dogs too have now really settled down – they apparently used to bark and howl a lot at night, seemingly for no reason, and sleeping was difficult. Perhaps, as various studies have shown, the renovation work triggered off the ghostly activity in the Morgan's home but one thing is for sure – they hope it never returns.

I have heard the theory put forward that ghostly activity following renovation work on period properties involves once more the stone tape recording effect readers will now be familiar with. If one supposes that the walls of a building can in some way record events, noises, etc. from the past, perhaps one way to trigger a playback is to jolt or hammer on these walls. This action could act as the switch, releasing the playback of sounds and images. Renovation work usually involves much hammering and banging on walls, and even in some cases the removal of walls. In many cases I have followed up regarding the sudden start-up of ghostly activity, building work or renovations to the building are a factor.

CASE 47 | FRED'S HAND

IT WAS a warm evening in mid-September and I was visiting my friends Paul and Sue Hopgood who had experienced a long-running haunting. I had been asked to help make a video to show viewers what a typical all-night ghostwatch entails. As Paul and Sue are both mediums, the video company wanted them to be present to give their overall impressions of any spiritual activity that might take place there.

I knocked on the door (the bell was not working) and Paul seemed a little flustered on answering. He said that some odd things had occurred that evening, and proceeded to tell me all about them. Earlier that evening, the family were surprised (to say the least!) by the back door opening on its own. The handle was turned by an invisible hand and a blast of air entered the room. Some time later, just when I had knocked at the front door, all the lights that were on in the house went off momentarily, only to come back on seconds later. Sue joked that 'Fred' (the affectionate name they have given to their particular ghost) was active that night.

The couple's youngest daughter, nine-year-old Heather, was sitting on the couch, snuggled up to her mother as she was feeling poorly with a slight fever. After Paul had brought me a drink, Heather asked me if I had been sunbathing. I laughed at this, as my last holiday had been some weeks earlier, and also since I rarely seem to have the time or indeed the patience for sunbathing. Paul told me that a large handprint had suddenly appeared on my chest and extended to the bottom of my throat. I did not believe him, so I went out into the hall and glanced in the mirror. I was taken aback to see a very large man's handprint on my neck. It was white and the surround of the print was livid red. I placed my own hand over the mark to see if somehow I had pressed my hand there myself and created the impression, but my own hand was far too small.

The oddest part about it all was that at no time after entering the house did I feel anything or anyone touch me at all. The only explanation I can come up with is that Fred wanted to make his presence felt and left his mark for all to see. I only regret not having taken my camera with me to record the incident.

The mark quickly faded and was completely gone the next day. At no time during my visit to my friends' house did I feel any unease at all – in fact quite the opposite. It would appear that their ghost has only the friendliest of intentions and didn't want to strangle me. He merely wanted to leave a tangible mark of his presence.

Weird events still keep happening in the home of Paul and Sue. The couple have, on occasion, left out a plate with iron filings on it in the kitchen. When they return to view the plate later, all sorts of swirling patterns have been created. Paul has assured me that this has happened many times when the house has been left empty. The couple believe that the iron filings are used by the spirit of Fred as a kind of artist's medium, and are one way of making his presence known. Interest in these activities has led to interviews for both German and Australian television.

CASE 48
COOMBE ABBEY – WEEKEND OF WEIRDNESS

THE BEAUTIFUL and magnificent grounds of Coombe Abbey, near Coventry (now a hotel and popular conference centre), make an ideal place to relax and soak up some of the religious history of Britain. Unfortunately, the splendid building is surrounded by modern housing estates that encroach on its peace and special kind of solemnity.

It is a truly massive estate, and as you drive up to the gates you are struck by the tree-lined grounds and the beautiful aspects in every direction. The deep and solemn moat is especially attractive. The building, with its central fountain, is equally dramatic.

Once inside, visitors become swallowed up into the medieval scene. Even the staff are dressed authentically. The numerous artifacts inside this former monastery are truly breathtaking. Busts of notaries gaze out serenely from their pedestals and exquisite tapestries recreate times long gone in vivid detail and colour. The sheer size and scale of the building are enough to leave you open-mouthed on occasion. There are so many objects of beauty and antiquity around it is a treat for the eye.

As I am a particular lover of history, when I visited Coombe Abbey with my family I found it extremely exciting. I felt like touching every statue, caressing the cool marble. I felt like touching each tapestry to feel the softness of the woven stitches. All this was almost too much temptation. As a hotel, it must rate as one of the most interesting in the world.

It was just before dinner and we were shown to our very sumptuous rooms, decorated very tastefully. These were comfortable and stylish in the extreme. The walls, several feet thick, added much to the atmosphere in the rooms. My son Laurie and his sisters decided to go off and explore the well-kept grounds and woodland. They went off eagerly, leaving me to collapse in a heap on the nearest available bed. A little overawed by the sheer beauty of the place, all I could think was that I must return soon.

It was nearly dinner time, and the hungry children rushed back eager for food and anticipating a good meal. Laurie then told me that near to the woods he had witnessed something strange. We were in a hurry, so I told him to elaborate on his experience later. He seemed a little breathless and worried, though this was not like him at all.

We sat down to a superb three-course meal. Then we went up to our rooms and flopped on our respective beds, tired from a long, exciting day.

The boys were in one room, and the girls in another. I didn't really expect to sleep well that night. In the middle hours of the night, when it was still dark, I heard a beautiful chanting, which sounded like Latin. I found it very comforting, and not frightening nor an annoyance.

However, as I am no expert I can only presume that the chanting is some sort of recorded memory of the past, possibly even captured in the very walls, and replayed back when the times are right. It soon sent me peacefully to sleep. I am a little unsure as to its origin: did it come directly from my room, or somewhere else?

Next day, I told my daughter Gemma about the singing monk and his soporific effect on me. She admitted that she had heard him too. He seemed to offer pure comfort, not meaning harm to those hearing his voice. I must say that I enjoyed his music greatly. We then tucked into a splendid full English breakfast and made the long drive back home, talking about the place where time stood still.

Some weeks later, Laurie divulged to me just what he had seen near the dense woods at Coombe Abbey. It was a hovering spaceship, like two saucers stuck together, with complicated symmetrical patterns on its sides. This young lad, who rates anything vaguely scientific as possible of future study, was afraid, and immediately rushed to tell either me or his father, but could not find us.

He vehemently believes that he saw an unexplained aircraft. Just why such a strange craft should hover for some time near to a medieval monastery is hard to fathom. It appears that no-one else witnessed the strange craft that day. I believe my son's account, and I can understand why it alarmed him. This case demonstrates the frequent proximity of UFO sightings and ghostly activity, a coincidence I find interesting.

WEIRD AND WONDERFUL

I N THIS section is a selection of stories hard to categorize but still worthy of inclusion. Some are horrific; others are almost funny. Most of
the people that came forward with the following encounters started
their dialogue with the famous words: 'You're not going to believe this,
but . . .'. In most cases, the witnesses were very reliable.

Ghostly activity is a broad subject and encompasses many things,
from brief and fleeting visions to all-out attack perpetrated by an
unfriendly poltergeist. It can include sounds, or touch, when nothing is
seen; or stigmata-type wounds can appear suddenly on a victim. In buildings, it can affect the temperature, create damp patches and flooding, and
even cause large-scale furniture to move about.

With so much diverse activity documented under the umbrella title
of 'ghosts', maybe it is wrong to be surprised, whatever happens.

CASE 49 THE BIBLE

I LIKE TO keep in touch, when I can, with the people I have met and
interviewed. Dean G's house in my home town of Northampton had
proved an interesting one. All sorts of phenomena had occurred there
over a long period: cold spots, disembodied voices, and a shadowy figure

in the bedroom pulling off the bedcovers, to name just three. The house is a Victorian cottage in a quiet back street.

Further developments were brought to light in a phone call from Dean one evening. He told me his brother-in-law had just given him an old Bible, the very large, leather-bound sort that would have been kept in the home with all the family births and deaths recorded in the front. Dean had purchased his house from his sister and her husband. Apparently, the Bible had been in the house originally, but had somehow got packed away during the move. The couple did not really want the book, and returned it to Dean as they felt it belonged in his house.

Dean phoned me to tell me about it, wondering if it could possibly affect the ghostly activity in his home. He told me it was a very ugly book, grey and dusty with gloomy engravings inside. When I went back to visit the house I noticed that the atmosphere seemed better. Dean was right about the Bible – it was not an attractive volume.

Normally, I really like old books, and I can remember the big old Bible we had at home when I was growing up. My mother had bought it from a secondhand shop, and she kept it under her bed. It was rarely opened up. However, the illustrations in our Bible could not have been more different; they were very beautiful, and most unlike those in Dean's copy.

Only time will tell if Dean's ghost remains quiet. Perhaps he or she was the original owner of the Bible and feels it is now back where it belongs. It is indeed a well-documented fact that in some hauntings, when an object belonging to a house is removed, then the disturbances can accelerate until the object is returned to its rightful place.

My cousin Sherry told me of just such a story. A friend of hers was renovating an old cottage. When opening up a sealed fireplace, she came across some delicate, but very dusty, antique, women's shoes. Unsure as to what to do with her find, the woman donated them to a local museum to put on display (Northampton is a town with a history of shoe-making). Within a short time, all hell broke loose in the poor woman's cottage. A friend suggested that maybe it was because she had moved the shoes. Apparently, in old houses sometimes small domestic items were buried in the hearth or under floorboards to protect the house from bad spirits, and bring it luck.

Very sceptical still, Sherry's friend kindly asked the museum for the return of her shoes and replaced them in their original spot in the fireplace. Peace was miraculously restored and the tiny shoes have not been moved since.

The exterior of Dean's house in Sharman Road.

CASE 50 AUNT LIZ

PHIL HILLIER from Wrexham has always been interested in ghosts. He told me of two experiences of his that are hard to dismiss as figments of the imagination, because at the time they seemed so real.

The first incident happened at work. Phil was working in the Department of Employment, which was based at the former Hightown Barracks in Wrexham. At the time, half of the barracks was still occupied by the army and half by the Department of Employment. The DOE occupied two buildings which were called Block 28 and Wynnstay Block. Phil was based at the latter.

Phil had not been working there long when he heard rumours that the barracks were haunted. A female colleague sitting next to Phil received a phone call from another staff member situated on the first level of Block 28, saying that the ghost was up and about again. Phil questioned the girl, who told him that the second level of Block 28 was unsafe and consequently nobody was based on that floor because it could not take the weight. Workers below could therefore tell when the ghost was up and about, as heavy footsteps were heard crossing the ceiling above. The ghost was purported to be that of a young soldier who hanged himself on the site.

It was a Friday morning when Phil had his first encounter with the ghost. He went to the toilet and, once inside the cubicle, shut the door. The next thing he knew was that the cubicle door was shaken extremely violently. This lasted for about 20 seconds. The shaking then stopped and started again, this time for longer. Immediately after this, Phil listened for footsteps, suspecting a prankster at work. On opening the door, he was surprised to see the toilet block empty of people.

Phil was also to see heavy doors to the offices opening and closing themselves, on many occasions. This could not be accounted for by draughts, as the weight of the doors made this impossible.

Phil's second and more vivid encounter happened in 1992. He heard that his great aunt Liz, who lived in south Wales, was about to pass away. The family always kept in touch by letter, and visited her at least once a year. It was the night after Phil had been told of his aunt's impending death that he experienced his ghostly encounter. Phil awoke to find what appeared to be his aunt Liz standing in the corner of the room. She was all in white. She called out his name and smiled. The following morning he was told that Liz had passed away in the night.

Everyone was upset and the journey to Margam Crematorium, south Wales, was a long and sad one. However, some weeks after the funeral, Phil's experience of seeing his late aunt was repeated. He did not feel at all afraid; rather, he felt a great warmth and peace and a certainty that she was there to say goodbye, for good this time. Aunt Liz has not been seen since by any of the family and they now believe her soul to be at peace.

Such (often nocturnal) one-off visits from a recently deceased loved one are extremely common: so common, in fact, that reports of them appear from every country on the globe year after year. This 'visit' is even incorporated into the bereavement period of some cultures. They expect the dead to return, and often have a meal laid out for the spirit, and candles lit. This belief system surely must help the family to come to terms with their loss, knowing for certain of an afterlife, and being in no fear of it for themselves.

CASE 51 | CAPTAIN BLOOD

IT WAS a dark, rainy night in 1991 when Tracey Thornton saw a mysterious figure in the road while driving home from work. It was about 3am. As Tracey approached the sharp bend along the quiet country road near the village of Boughton in Northamptonshire, she saw a man crouching in the middle of the road. Slamming on her brakes, and terrified that she would hit him, she was amazed when, on opening her clenched-up eyes, the road appeared to be completely empty. Frightened and shaking, she quickly drove the rest of the way home 'like a bat out of hell', as she put it.

She gave the matter some thought over the following weeks and was always a bit nervous when driving along the same stretch of road, hoping that her experience would not be repeated. However, this was not to be the case. Incredibly, about three years later, Tracey, a friend and her sister Kerry were driving along the same stretch of road. It was late at night once again, between midnight and 1am. The girls were all in good spirits and chatting and laughing on their way home together in the car, when they saw a man suddenly run across the road ahead, straight into the front of the car.

Naturally, they were all astonished to see him disappear into the side of the vehicle on impact, almost as if the solid car did not exist. He just went straight through the side of it. The thing that shocked them most, however, was not the fact that they had just seen a ghost but that for Tracey it was the second time. The man running across the road and the crouching person seen three years earlier were one and the same. She described him to me as aged about 30, dressed in long, dark, leather, over-the-knee boots, grey trousers and a white, ruffled shirt. His hair was dark and he appeared to be totally unaware of the cars on the road.

The lane where the phantom is regularly seen running across the road.

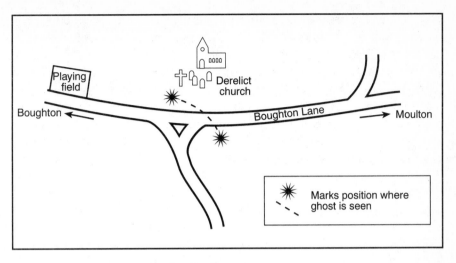

The route taken by Captain Blood's ghost.

Seeking some sort of rational explanation for the ghostly encounters, Tracey looked into the history of the area and she discovered a local legend about the place. The man is known as 'Captain Blood', and has reputedly been seen by many of the locals on the road which runs past the deserted, crumbling cemetery there. The church on the site is now just a decaying ruin, with many of the gravestones toppled over and broken, or sadly overgrown with tangled weeds. The ruined church and graveyard are indeed very atmospheric. The place also has rumours of witchcraft attached to it. Unfortunately, this is the fate experienced by many quiet, deserted graveyards.

CASE 52 TWO CHILDREN

ONE SUMMER evening in 1996, 13-year-old Ruth Whysall encountered the ghost of a child peering around the door of her spare bedroom. Ruth told me that her house used to be the old swimming pool bath house in Radnor, Derbyshire. Because of this, she wondered if perhaps it was the ghost of a child who drowned in the pool a generation earlier.

Ruth's house itself is fairly new but is built on the foundations of the old pool. It was about 9pm when she saw the figure, which seemed like a dense, black shadow. Although she initially felt calm, once she realized what she had seen, she (in her own words) 'ran scared up to my room, jumped into bed and hid under the covers in shock!'

When she asked her parents about it the next morning, they were understandably a bit sceptical. No-one else had seen the ghost, and they knew nothing of the history of the house. The incident will therefore probably remain unsolved. Was it simply a shadow, the rest just the fill-in of a teenager's overactive imagination? Or was it indeed the ghost of a child who had died there some time in the past, that could only be seen by the open and unquestioning gaze of another child?

Ruth has never forgotten her encounter with the ghost of the little girl, and is sure of what she saw. This case once more appears to be a type of recording or place memory, by far the most common of all paranormal sightings, but interesting nevertheless.

CASE 53 THE MAN WITHOUT A FACE

IT WAS October 1951 and Ron Dartnell was on his way back to the airforce camp near Andover in Hampshire on his motorbike. It was fairly late and quite dark. The only illumination was the full moon and the lights of his bike. As the village of Hurstbourne Tarrant came into sight, the motorbike engine spluttered and slowed right down. Ron was annoyed and concerned, as he still had some miles to go. He was just about to stop and take a look at the engine, when he happened to glance to his side.

At the top of the hill, some yards to the right, was an old-fashioned, black stagecoach going along at some speed. Ron was very puzzled. He said the vehicle put him in mind of the sort of coach from the days of Dick Turpin. There was no sound discernible above the failing motorbike engine, and Ron looked and looked again at the apparition. Suddenly, the coach just seemed to disappear; at the same time, his bike roared back to life. He made his way back to camp.

After talking about the incident with his mates back at camp, one of them told him that an old coaching road, now disused, ran parallel with the modern road, and it was on this thoroughfare that Ron had witnessed the coach. He was to make that same journey many times later on, but the experience was never repeated.

It was over 30 years later when Ron had his second experience of the supernatural. Ron went to fetch his 16-year-old son Kevin from the scout hut at Overstone near Northampton. It was approximately 10pm. As the car park in front of the hut was full, he parked near some trees, keeping his eye out for Kevin leaving.

After sitting quietly for about ten minutes, Ron began to feel very cold. He glanced out of the driver's window and saw the shadowy figure of a man bending down to look into the car at him. The most terrifying thing that Ron noticed was the absence of a face. Instead, there was just a dark void under the man's hat. The figure was wearing some sort of raincoat, or a loose, smock-like coat, and a hat not dissimilar to those worn by Canadian Mounties. (Ron was later to find out that in previous times scout masters wore similar hats.) Terrified, Ron started up the car and drove away from the trees, right up to the scout hall where it was light, to wait for his son. Sylvia, his wife, told me that Ron was so shaken up on his return home that his face was pallid and white.

There is a local legend associated with Overstone scout camp. It concerns a young scout who died there and is said to wander the grounds at night. Numerous people in cars who have come across the lad have been shocked when the car headlights have shone straight through him.

Ron Dartnell still finds it difficult to believe in the possibility of ghostly apparitions, yet he cannot deny what he saw on those two evenings 30 years apart.

CASE 54 A SENSE OF ALARM

OCCASIONALLY, unexplained phenomena disrupt the mundane routine of work. This was true in Simon N's case. What makes this case particularly interesting is that the effects were corroborated by a number of other people. Simon N now lives in Bristol and currently works for the social services as an officer in charge of a centre for adults

with learning difficulties. The first incident happened when he was working and living in Derbyshire.

Simon worked in a residential hostel, often spending the night on
duty there; even though he went to bed, he slept with a 'buzzer', as he
had to be prepared to get up during the night to deal with any emergency. At about 3am on the night in question, his buzzer went off, and
Simon quickly dressed and went to investigate. He found Julia, the night-
care aide, in the staffroom looking worried and a little embarrassed. She
apologized for waking him as there had been no actual emergency, but
explained that she had been frightened to see lights coming on in a part
of the building known to be empty and unused.

From the staff room, it was possible to see across a small courtyard
to a unit of the building that had been unoccupied for some time.
Suspecting an intruder, Simon told his workmate to stay in the staff room
while he investigated. The unit was duly searched and, surprisingly,
found to be empty. All the lights were off. As Simon walked across the
courtyard, he remarked to Julia that he felt this was puzzling. Within
minutes the two were amazed when, looking back across the courtyard,
they saw that the lights were back on again. At this point they were both
quite frightened by the situation, but Simon went back once again and
re-checked the empty building, looking under all the beds and in all of
the cupboards.

The incident was duly reported in the morning and an electrician
called in to check the wiring system. It was found to be in full working
order, and the electrician was at a complete loss to explain the previous
evening's events.

This part of the building is now used once more, but staff still report
strange happenings there. Light bulbs 'pop' with such regularity that
electricians are frequently called to check the circuits – no abnormality
has ever been discovered. Empty rooms have also been found to be
locked from the inside and staff have had to use a screwdriver to enter
them. During these incidents, the windows have always been firmly shut,
making it impossible for an outsider to enter the rooms and lock the
doors from the inside.

However, it was the short-term care unit in Derbyshire where Simon
worked that was known to be most 'haunted'. The staff here have almost
got used to the phenomena, and now generally take them for granted. As
the name implies, the short-term care unit has no permanent residents,
its purpose being to provide respite care for people with learning difficulties. Some years ago, in one of the bedrooms, a young woman had a

fit and died during the night. She was a woman who displayed compulsive routines, and her ghost is said to continue with this behaviour.

Simon's encounter with her ghost happened when he had only just started working in that part of the building and he did not know anything of its history. It was teatime and Simon, another member of staff and all the residents of the unit were sitting down to tea in the dining room. From where he was seated, Simon had a clear view through the doorway into the corridor that led to the bedrooms. As he passed the food round, he glimpsed a slim woman, dressed in light brown, walking down the corridor and into one of the bedrooms.

As everyone in the building was present in the dining room, Simon went to enquire after the woman, in case she had come to visit someone at the unit and was lost. Entering the room, he saw it was empty, but all the towels from the other rooms had been folded into squares and piled neatly onto the bed. When he mentioned this puzzling experience to his colleagues, they told him of the story of a girl who had died in that bedroom, room 16. Apparently one of her peculiar obsessive habits when she was at the hostel was to tidy up and stack all the towels.

Simon told me of another ghostly resident at the hostel. At one time, a girl called Amy had spent a lot of time there. She was a very dominant personality, but very popular with the staff in spite of her childlike, disruptive behaviour. One of her favourite pranks was to set off all the fire alarms and revel in the havoc that ensued.

One night, a few weeks after Amy had left the hostel, all the fire alarms went off simultaneously. Staff evacuated the buildings and the fire brigade was called out. No fire was discovered and there was no obvious fault in the system; the incident remained a mystery until the next morning, when staff received the news that Amy had died during the night. It was later confirmed that she had died at the exact time that the alarms went off. It was as if Amy had wanted to let her friends know of her death by triggering all the alarms, a nuisance she had often perpetrated in life.

Simon tells me he is at a loss to explain all the ghostly goings-on at the social security hostel, a building which only dates back to the early 1980s. Some delving into the history of the site brought to light the fact that the hostel was built on the site of two much older buildings that were demolished. In addition, running directly underneath is an underground stream. (There has been a tentative connection, suggested among certain parapsychologists, between ghostly and paranormal activity and the proximity to a ley line or an underground stream or water source. Maybe, however, it is due to the two premature deaths that occurred there.

CASE 55 BROWNSEA ISLAND

DAVE B, who hails from Weymouth in Dorset, but now lives in the Midlands, and is in his 40s, told me of his two experiences of ghosts. The first happened in the 1970s when he worked as a kitchen porter. His place of work was a castle-turned-hotel on Brownsea Island in the middle of Poole harbour in Dorset. The island is a haven for wildlife and has its own nature trail. The castle is owned by a major high street retailer, who uses the hotel as a holiday location for its staff.

It was August and for three weeks there was a spate of strange occurrences: some of the female workers saw the former lady owner of the castle, then deceased, walking in the grounds. However, it was Dave and two co-workers who were frightened one night by doors slamming near the room that they all shared. It woke them up and, at first, logically, they thought it was just a fierce draught. But then, when Dave got up to investigate, the door to their room opened and slammed shut loudly. Suspecting a prankster, Dave leapt for the door, only to open it and reveal an empty corridor. The three men were surprised, to say the least, by their sudden unexpected awakening, but could offer up no explanations, except that maybe the castle was haunted after all.

Dave B's second incident happened when he was married to his first wife and had just moved into a newly built house at Standens Barn, Northampton. One evening he was sitting in the lounge relaxing and reading the paper, when he heard footsteps cross the room and the kitchen door open. He presumed that his wife had gone to make tea, and was surprised when after about five minutes the kitchen light had not been turned on.

He went into the kitchen, but it was empty. Just then his wife came down from upstairs where she had been having a lie down. Dave told me he is at a total loss to explain the invisible intruder in the house that day. If it was indeed a ghost of some kind, he cannot understand why, as the house was brand new and presumably had no history of former owners.

One possibility is that someone walked into the wrong house by mistake, as it was a new estate; or an intruder entered the house hoping to steal something quickly and get away, not caring too much that there were people in there. We shall never know, but I like to keep an open mind on this one.

56 CULLODEN

O N 16 APRIL 1996, Corinne P and her two friends were visiting the site of the Battle of Culloden, on its 250th anniversary. Over 5,000 people were to visit the site, and television and radio crews covered the event; people had come from all over the world, especially those whose relatives had fallen there.

Corinne P took many photographs while she was there. When she developed them, in one she noticed in the grass the image of a face. It appeared to be that of a man wearing a hat reminiscent of the 'bonnets' worn by Highland soldiers at the time of the battle. Her interest aroused, Corinne borrowed a number of books from the library, hoping to find out more about the battle.

Corinne and her friend Denise sat looking at the books in the kitchen for a while and then, leaving them in a pile on the kitchen table, they went into the lounge for coffee. On returning to the kitchen, Corinne was amazed to see one of the books standing upright on the kitchen floor, opened and with one page folded in half to the spine. The page concerned depicted a Highlander in traditional dress.

Denise picked up the book, as Corinne was too frightened to do so, and replaced it on the pile on the table. Both women knew that the book had mysteriously moved in their absence, as they knew where they had left it earlier.

After the incident, Corinne noticed a strange atmosphere in the kitchen, and as her husband was away working she was scared. Something had entered her home and she was perplexed as to what it was. Other things were moved about and disturbed in the kitchen over the following weeks and it soon become a bit too much to cope with.

One day, some time after the book incident, Corinne and her neighbour were in the lounge chatting, when the subject of the photo came up again. Suddenly the two women heard a scratching noise, rather like fingernails scraping against the back of a stiff hessian carpet. At first they thought it might be the cat crunching on her biscuits, but on glancing into the kitchen they could see her lying asleep on the windowsill outside.

The noise got louder and louder, until the women could not hear their own voices above it. They became very frightened, and Corinne shouted 'Stop that now!' Immediately, the noise stopped. Cautiously, the two women stepped into the kitchen, unsure what to expect there. The atmosphere in the room felt horrible. They looked around to see what could have made the awful noise. The neighbour looked under the table and saw the rough wood underneath it. She scraped at this with her nails. It made exactly the same sound that they had heard, albeit a lot quieter. Clearly, something had been in the kitchen seconds before, scratching at the table and trying to get their attention.

After this, Corinne sought help and advice from a medium from Edinburgh, who had previously seen the photo taken by Corinne at Culloden and sensed that it depicted a man killed there. As his restless spirit had been trying to find peace, the soldier had remained on the battle site ever since. Visiting Corinne's home later, the psychic felt the spirit had followed Corinne home and had been desperately trying to attract her attention, sensing her to be a very sympathetic person. The psychic performed a sort of exorcism in the kitchen and felt the ghost of the man leave by the open back door. Nothing unusual occurred thereafter.

The photograph concerned was sent to ASSAP (a scientific body that studies all kinds of phenomena) and they judged it to be an example of simulacra (human faces and forms seen in natural formations), as indeed I did after analysing the picture. However coincidental this was, I believe that Corinne did experience a poltergeist type of infestation after her visit to the Culloden site. She told me she did feel extremely moved by the visit, as she thinks relatives on her mother's side of the family lost their lives at the Battle of Culloden 250 years ago.

Cases of simulacra are very commonplace; one paranormal journal has a regular photo spot devoted to this subject each month. Rocks, trees, bushes and even clouds have been known to produce formations or effects that resemble human faces or the human form.

CASE 57 | VOICES FROM THE DEAD

IN 1997, Simon, from the pretty Northamptonshire village of Fosters Booth, told me about a frightening experiment he had once conducted. Simon, who is interested in both advanced mathematics and radio technology, decided to experiment, using his own radio, after reading of the work of Konstantin Raudive, a researcher in EVP (electric voice phenomena) whose experiments are described below.

To do this (usually when he was alone late in the evening and his wife Beryl was in bed), Simon would tune in his radio to frequencies in between stations until it produced 'white noise', that irritating sound that is not unlike bees buzzing or electrical humming. Then he set up a tape-recorder to record any sounds produced – paranormal or otherwise. Playing back his recording of the white noise later, he was somewhat disappointed, but not too surprised, to hear none of the 'voices' reported by Raudive.

Not one to give up easily, Simon tried one more time, more out of boredom than anything else. To his complete surprise, listening to the second tape he heard, albeit with difficulty, a voice. It was unfamiliar and the words could not easily be deciphered, but the voice sounded like that of a male speaking in a low flat tone.

Next day, rather excited, he told Beryl about it and she also listened to the tape. She could hear the strange voice, but it frightened her. She told Simon to stop his stupid experiments, saying it wasn't right to attempt communication with the dead. Beryl found the whole thing very unsettling, but being a calm, no-nonsense sort of woman she soon forgot all about it.

Simon didn't, and a few weeks later he began the experiment again in earnest. This time, he told me, he had almost unbelievable success in taping the voices. He obtained many voices over a period of months. They gradually became clearer (or perhaps he had just become better at deciphering the words). At first, the messages were quite benign, even friendly, purporting to be from deceased persons. Telling of an afterlife, they appeared grateful to Simon for providing a channel through which they could pass on information.

Soon, he told me, this practice became highly addictive, proving almost impossible to stop. With the passage of time, however, the voices changed. They became more like nasty gossips, tormenting Simon about factors he was unhappy with in his own life and those of his neighbours. The voices, usually male, told him of a local farmer he knew and his long-running affair. This surprised him.

The gossip got more and more personal in nature, and was quite hard to listen to. He found that long after listening to the tapes the nasty words and accusations were hard to forget. He quickly became depressed and lost weight. This was noticed by his wife, who was horrified when he explained the reason for it. Beryl had thought the experiments had ended months before.

Sensibly, she demanded that he stop and, gathering all of his tapes together, she angrily threw them into the bin. Gradually, Simon's health improved, and he told me that he has not resumed his former foolish activities, and never will. He feels sure that negative spirits used his radio set to come through. They passed on information that, if it had been mentioned to others (which is what they seemed to want), could have caused real upset and even devastated people's lives. The practice of listening to the voices eventually became an obsession, leading to Simon's own ill health.

Obviously sceptics would totally disbelieve that such a process is possible, and would say it was simply a case of an overactive imagination hearing among the white noise exactly what he wanted to hear, that is a sort of aural hallucination. They would argue that Simon caused his own depression and accompanying anxiety by the use of his own imagination and fears.

I can't say, as personally I have never tried such an experiment, but I am aware of others' work in this field. As well as Konstantin Raudive, who died in 1974, there were the earlier discoveries of Swede Friedrich Jurgenson and his now-famous 1959 tapes of forest birdsong and accompanying anomalous voices. Raudive, a former student of Jung, began to make his own recordings, wanting to see if it was possible using radio technology to communicate with the dead. He made in total over 100,000 tapes under strict laboratory conditions. About 206 distinct voices appeared. They spoke using short sentences and an odd rhythm. Others listened to these tapes and could clearly make out at least 27 of them. They made statements such as 'The dead live' and 'I am alive, Konstantin', often sounding surprised at being disturbed in this way. Raudive, who was a devout Catholic all his life, informed the Vatican of his discoveries. They showed a sympathetic interest in the 'voice phenomena'. Other eminent researchers since have followed on with this work, obtaining mixed results.

In Simon's case, I believe the radio set to have acted a little like a Ouija board, attracting some good but ultimately bad spirit communicators. This can only cause distress and upset, and so I would strongly discourage anyone from experimenting in this way, because who knows what they could hear. Words are often hard to forget, and cruel ones particularly so.

CASE
58 WORKMATES

TRINA F, from the Whitehills area of Northampton, told me recently of her friend Elaine's encounter with a ghost, the ghost of her mother. Trina's mother had died over ten years earlier from cancer. She had struggled long and hard against the disease but eventually succumbed, leaving Trina to bring up her much younger brother John.

One day Trina was in town shopping when she unexpectedly bumped into Elaine (Elaine's mother and Trina's mother had worked together years before) Elaine seemed a bit subdued, and told her friend about her mother's death.

Trina was upset by this and offered her sympathies. However, Elaine quickly replied that it was all right now and not to worry as Trina's mother had told her everything would be OK. This puzzled Trina, as her own mother had died years before. Seeing Trina's puzzled face, Elaine explained.

After her own mother's lingering death, she was of course very upset and was finding it very hard to come to terms with it all. Then one night she had a particularly vivid dream. In this dream Trina's mother came to her and told her everything was fine and that the two former workmates were together again. They would look after one another. This had evidently made the death easier to bear.

Trina laughed when she related this story to me. She said, 'That is just like Mum. She always said that if she could come back with a message she would. She truly believed in life after death and that it was entirely possible for us to communicate with loved ones in the afterlife.'

Although this is not a ghost story in the strictest sense, as the vision occurred during sleep, it illustrates an aspect of ghostly phenomena that is little documented, that of information from the dead passed on to us during our dreams. I have heard of cases where the dead have appeared in dreams (a bit like an extra in a television programme), popping in unexpectedly to relay an important message, such as a warning of danger ahead, or to tell the bereaved person exactly where to find a ring that is lost, for example, or perhaps a will that is proving elusive to locate.

Whether this is our subconscious mind set loose by sleep, giving us information we knew already but had forgotten, is hard to tell. Whatever the cause of this type of dream may be, 'ghost' dreams are universal, and as such I feel they are worthy of further study.

PHANTOM PHANTOMS

UNFORTUNATELY, ANY paranormal investigator will encounter many of these in the course of their work. Some ghosts turn out to be anything but. The human mind is very capable of conjuring up almost anything, and it is very easy to be mistaken. Old houses with creaking floorboards, noisy ancient plumbing and draughty rooms can be behind many so-called ghostly phenomena. Hoaxers can also never be ruled out when investigating a haunting. When a 'haunting' chiefly involves children, it can often be a form of attention-seeking that can quickly be spotted.

Of course, ardent sceptics would say that 100 per cent of ghost encounters are hoaxes or mistakes. There is no convincing these. Without personal, first-hand experience, it is difficult to turn any sceptic into a believer. However, if only 1 per cent of all the incidents that get reported to researchers like me are genuine, then this would turn much scientific thinking on its head. Survival of death, telekinesis and precognition would all be real possibilities, as I believe them to be.

The implications of this would be huge, particularly if they could be proven beyond scientific doubt and replicated in the laboratory. That time is not too many years ahead, I hope. All any investigator can try to do is separate the wheat from the chaff. Some examples of the 'chaff' are included in this section.

THE HEADLESS ORGANIST

SOME YEARS ago Neil D was working in a Northamptonshire cinema. At the time some renovation work was being undertaken there. One evening, after the workmen had left, Neil and a friend were just about to lock up. One of them glanced over towards the organ (left over from the long-gone days of the silent films) and was shocked to see a headless, gowned figure sitting at the organ. Plucking up courage, Neil slowly approached, determined to get a closer look. As he got closer, Neil could not help but laugh: the headless figure turned out to be a discarded newspaper slung on the chair by one of the workmen earlier in the day. Somehow, it had formed itself into a conical shape and, in the dim light of the cinema, appeared torso-like.

I wonder whether, if Neil had not been brave enough to approach the 'ghost', perhaps a tale would have been told of the headless organist of the cinema. Of such stuff are legends made.

Neil told me of another weird experience that he had as a lad that he could find no explanation for. In his bedroom he had some new linoleum fitted (in those days fitted carpet was rare). One night he got undressed and jumped into bed, having placed his shoes where he always did, in front of the chest of drawers. In the morning, he got up and dressed ready for breakfast. Neil picked up his shoes and was shocked to see two perfect imprints of them where they had stood overnight. He told his parents, worried that he might be in trouble for spoiling the lino. The imprints stayed there until some years later when his room was carpeted.

Thinking about it, Neil wondered about the cause. He is sure that he had not trodden in any chemicals or anything similar. Surely, if that had been the case the rest of the house would have shown signs of it too.

This strange story reminds me of a case I read about that happened in an office in America. After a thunder storm the night before, workers found on the polished wooden floorboards the imprint of a wicker wastepaper basket. Experts thought it was a rare example of spontaneous natural photography caused by the lightning. Perhaps there was a thunderstorm the night Neil's shoes were captured on the lino like the footprints of a phantom.

CASE 60   THE GHOST THAT WASN'T

MIKE, A professional photographer by trade who lives in the village of Moulton in Northamptonshire, passed on what at first sight seemed an interesting photograph to me, via a mutual friend. The picture showed the indistinct figure of a man sitting on a sofa. It was taken around Christmas time in 1996.

Mike had related the story of how he came to take the picture of the 'ghost' to my friend. He told him that, since moving into his semi-detached house with his wife and children, on many occasions he had seen the ghost of an elderly gentleman appear on the sofa in the lounge. Such was the regularity of the phenomenon that he had a loaded camera at the ready one day. In the few seconds that the gentleman appeared, he was able to get his shot.

The double-exposure fake ghost photograph created by Mike.

I was quite excited at first by the photograph as, obviously, pictures of this type are very few and far between. However, when my friend questioned Mike further and mentioned possible inclusion of his photograph in a book, Mike admitted that it was a fake. Initially, he had done it for a laugh. It was actually a double-exposure shot: he had taken a picture of the room with himself sitting down and then quickly vacated the sofa so that only a misty impression of a sitting figure was left in the photograph.

This case illustrates two things: firstly, how easy it is for someone, especially a photographer, to fake a picture; secondly, that people have many reasons for trying to fake pictures of ghosts – it might be for a joke or even in the hope of fame and financial reward. Any serious researcher into the paranormal must always be on their guard for such a scenario. If something seems too good to be true, it probably is!

I am glad that I found out that Mike's picture was a fake before I published it. Once something is in print, it is very difficult to retract your former views on it. I, like anyone else, hate to make mistakes. Almost anyone with a working knowledge of photography can mock up a double exposure which looks realistic.

CASE 61 THE HUTCHISON EFFECT

I WAS MOST fortunate in meeting the now well-known scientist Albert Budden in November 1997. We were both appearing on the same television show. Chatting over coffee before our interviews, we discovered that we were involved in research into similar areas. I was to be on the show to talk about the bizarre effect I seem to exert over electrical equipment when I go near it or touch it, and Albert was the expert discussing his theories on so-called 'electrosensitive people', research he has been involved in for over 15 years.

We discussed our both working on various poltergeist cases and he told me of a relatively new breakthrough in science that could go some way to explain the phenomenon. In the early 1980s, a Canadian physicist called Hutchison created in his workshop a huge machine using a veritable mishmash of equipment that generated large opposing electrical and magnetic fields.

The Canadian was amazed, when his machine was up and running, at the strange effects it exerted over a random selection of objects placed in the vicinity. Bowls were seen to levitate, planks of wood stood on end by themselves, and yoghurt slurped out of a pot. Even fairly large metal objects were moved by a seemingly invisible force. Many of them were permanently bent.

All of this might seem to belong in the realm of fiction, but it has been captured for everyone to see on video. Spontaneous fires would break out and extinguish themselves, and sparks and flashes of light also appeared. What Hutchison seems to have achieved in his laboratory is the recreation of many of the aspects of the poltergeist phenomenon, simply by using the forces of electricity and magnetism in a previously uncombined form.

I had read about Hutchison's work and Albert's involvement with it a couple of months before, and I found the whole thing to be very exciting. Any researcher worth their salt should be pleased when another part of the puzzle is put into place, whatever their field of research, and I really feel that Albert and the Canadian Hutchison have stumbled on a quite momentous discovery.

The crux of Albert's work, however, is the uncovering of the hidden environmental hazard of electromagnetic fields generated by electricity pylons, microwave ovens, televisions, industry and telephones, for example. He told me that some people seem to become hypersensitive to the constant bombardment of these fields, and this results in peculiar effects, both on the recipient's body and on electrical items around them. The sufferer can become very ill over a period of time as the body desperately tries to fight against the effects. Disorders of glands such as the thyroid, pancreas and adrenals are common, as are migraines and episodes of amnesia. The sufferer also disrupts and can even destroy electrical goods that they touch. This happens as the hypersensitive person seems to store up electricity rather like a human battery, and then, at times of stress, discharges it all in a flash. This overloads the electrical appliance, computer or television and often causes it to explode.

This seems almost ridiculous, even funny. However, when it happens on a regular basis, as indeed it did to me, it becomes less of a joke and more of an expensive bind. Since our meeting, I have read up more on Albert's extensive work and I can only express a sense of admiration at the sheer thoroughness and dedication of the man to his chosen field.

CASE 62 ECTOPLASM

LIONEL BEER from Middlesex sent me an interesting photograph. He was not sure what it portrayed, but thought it was possibly ghostly in origin. He told me it was taken in June 1992 on a field trip.

Lionel and some friends had stopped off for lunch in a pub – he is unsure of the name – along the Kennet and Avon canal (crop circle country). A friend had taken several pictures that day and when they came back from the developers one of them was particularly curious. It appears to show Mr Beer surrounded by a mist-like vapour, not unlike the ectoplasm so often produced by Victorian mediums during séances. You can just about make out the chin and hand of Mr Beer behind it all.

I had the photograph analysed, however, by an expert, who concluded it was probably a case of a sticky camera shutter and the camera being moved while the photo was taken. The swathes of white mist were caused by a white object or light source initially, which when the camera moved produced the mist-like effect. Apparently this can happen with an old or seldom-serviced camera. However, Mr Beer told me that all the other photographs in the reel of film came out normally.

Since viewing Lionel Beer's photograph, coincidentally I have come across many others like it. Some have been sent to me, and others have been published in newspapers and magazines. It is always a disappointment to come across possible photographic evidence, only to have it quickly explained away by a photographic expert. The genuine article – a ghost on film – remains astonishingly rare, considering that the camera has been with us for over a century.

CASE 63 GHOSTS OF THE GARDEN VARIETY

OCCASIONALLY I have been fortunate enough to hear about local hauntings worthy of investigation. In this next example, however, it turned out to be a bit of a wild goose chase. I have only recounted it here because it helps to demonstrate that much of any ghost hunter's job is spent following up stories that turn out either to be totally untrue or just plain misunderstandings and a waste of time. This ghost 'haunting' turned out, however, to be quite funny.

One day my sister-in-law Linda told me about an old lady known by a friend of hers. Apparently, the old lady was employed at a local farmhouse as a cleaner. She had worked there for years and told anyone who wanted to listen about the odd goings-on there. Things had been seen moving on their own, so she reckoned the place was haunted. I was given her phone number and rang her up the next day.

As she was rather deaf, she asked me to speak up. I carefully explained to her that I was writing a book on ordinary people's experiences of ghosts and had heard that she had experienced things of that nature that might be worth following up. Sounding confused, she replied that she knew absolutely nothing on the subject and that I would be far better off talking to her neighbour, as she had two in her garden.

Perplexed now, I asked her to explain further. She said, 'Oh yes, they're lovely angoras you know'. Suddenly I understood. She had misheard and thought I had said I was writing a book about *goats*. She got quite cross when I started laughing, and I had to put the phone down. Somehow, I think a book about ordinary people's experiences of goats would not sell quite as many copies...

CASE 64 | CLIVE'S GHOST

SOMETIMES OUR imaginations can literally almost scare us to death. This is true of the next case. It was early 1997 and Dave and his sister Marcie visited my house. Marcie said she was very worried about her brother and wondered if I could help. They both knew of my work as a paranormal investigator, and also that on occasion I worked as a medium. They hoped that just maybe I could understand their problem enough to be able to resolve it for them.

Dave runs his own business and works hard, but for many months he had been plagued by frightening thoughts. The only boy in a family of four girls, he was not, as one might have expected, his father's favourite. His father was a strict ex-army disciplinarian, inclined to be cruel on occasion to his only son. He was a man who developed a lifelong fascination with the occult, and claimed to have special powers. He had once told his son that he would come back and haunt him after death, and this is what a very nervous Dave believed to be happening.

He told me that his job made it necessary sometimes to be alone in empty buildings, doing rewiring. It was at these times that he sensed acutely the presence of his father, still angry at him for childhood mis-demeanours. It was all really starting to get to Dave and wear him down. He slept poorly and was nervous of being on his own.

As he laughingly told me, this was slightly ridiculous for a grown man. He had all his life been terrified by the thought of ghosts, however, so to believe that the spirit of his father was following him around as a kind of tormentor was too much to bear.

Marcie leant across the table and showed me a photograph of her father Clive. He was a grey-haired gentleman with glasses and intelligent eyes. Marcie said that she had never been afraid of him like Dave had. Being his daughter, he had treated her more kindly, and in many ways had been a good father.

She had brought the photograph along, hoping I could pick something up from it. I told the brother and sister that I needed to take the picture into a quiet room and concentrate on it, to see what thoughts on their unusual dilemma came to me. I went into the next room, carefully holding the photograph.

Sitting in a comfortable chair, I relaxed and asked questions in my mind of the man in the picture. Was he bothering his son? If so, why? I asked these two questions over and over in my head. After about five minutes, I clearly pictured this man, Clive. Their father had his back to me at first and was laughing. Then he slowly turned around and said, 'Tell Dave not to be so stupid and pull himself together. I haven't come back, you know, and I don't intend to. I love my son, but just tell him from me to get on with his life as he should.'

The image quickly faded and I went back into the dining room to the pair sitting anxiously at the table. I placed the photograph back on the table and repeated the message that I had received, word for word. Marcie seemed astonished. It was just how her father would have spoken to her brother, swearing at him one minute, but still telling him that he loved him.

Dave started to look a little reassured at this. I told him the idea of his father's ghost haunting him had somehow been implanted in his mind. It was a false and destructive thought, but with his new knowledge it would soon go. He had to believe in the falsity of these thoughts and in the truth that his father was dead and held no grudge against his son.

Marcie picked up her photograph to pop it back into her bag, and took an audible sharp inward breath. 'Oh my God, look, the photo has changed.' I didn't quite believe it, but looking at it I realized that the gentleman's glasses had misted up, like they do when the person has been crying or is in the bath.

This obviously scared Marcie. I wondered aloud at first if perhaps it was simply my fingerprints, hot from concentration, that had left their mark on the picture if I had inadvertently touched it. So I tried pressing hard with my fingers on another two points on the picture's edge, before removing them. The same effect was not achieved. So it hadn't been me.

I said to Marcie that perhaps it was some sort of physical sign that contact with her dead father had been made; and rather than worry about it they could view it as confirmation of all I had said to them. I asked her to place the photograph between the pages of the family Bible, if they had one, and leave it for a few days. I felt sure that when she next looked it would be totally back to normal.

They left reassured, and the next day I received a phone call from a happier Dave. He had slept like a log that night. It took him a couple of weeks to dismiss the frightening thoughts of his father. He no longer has them. Marcie looked at the photograph some time later and her father's glasses were clear.

This case demonstrates how powerful our thoughts can become, even taking on a life of their own. Such thoughts can be very destructive and I believe Dave was heading for a possible breakdown if he hadn't conquered his fears. Talking always helps, as in a way it exorcises the demons that we construct for ourselves in the mind.

CASE 65 THE 'RICHARD AND JUDY' SHOW

IN SPRING 1997, Albert Budden and I had been asked to talk on a well-known daytime British television programme often referred to as the 'Richard and Judy' show. We were to be on almost last, and so we had to wait quite a long time in the 'green room'. Waiting around is awful if you are at all nervous; it's far better to go on at the beginning as you have less time to get worked up.

For once, on this occasion I was very nervous, and so by the time we went on air I'd got myself in quite a state. We sat in two armchairs opposite the famous couple. I was clutching a copy of my first book, determined to get in a plug for it if I could. Richard and Judy tried to put us at our ease; nevertheless I felt terrible. The filming started and I was asked many of the sorts of questions I'd become quite used to being asked by the media, such as what were the odd effects that I sometimes exerted over electrical items, light bulbs, vacuum cleaners and various other paraphernalia.

Then they turned to Albert and asked him about the 'Hutchison' effect (see Case 61) and what possible effect it could have on people and their environment. Richard made a half-hearted joke about the weirdness of it all. As I placed my book on the table, quite without warning two things happened almost simultaneously. The first was that, while he was in mid-sentence, Albert's front tooth, which is capped, fell out. Cleverly, and as dexterously as a conjuror in the middle of a trick, he caught it in his hand and hid it in a tissue. Then the electronically operated blinds at the large picture window, near to where we sat, slid down by themselves and stopped working.

Richard commented on this and jokingly said, 'I think, Natalie, that you've just caused our blinds to malfunction.' It seemed that Albert's theories of the Hutchison effect had just been demonstrated on live television. I wonder if the high electrical fields in the studio, with all the lights and cameras, coupled with my nerves and agitation that morning, somehow (if telekinesis is a reality) caused this minor havoc.

After the interview, Albert and I shook hands with the presenters (I think Judy was a bit scared to do this in case she got a shock) and we made our way back to the green room for a cup of tea. Albert then told me how he'd felt his jaw vibrate when he sat down next to me in the studio. The next thing he knew was that the tooth had shot out. It was an expensive dentistry job, too, being a false enamel tooth attached by a screw to the jaw. He subsequently had to have his tooth re-attached, and I hoped that he wouldn't send me the bill.

It was a relief that it was all over, but I felt that I had made a real mess of the interview. The chaos at the studio reminded me of the chaos at the radio station in Northampton 18 months earlier. Maybe it was just a coincidence.

Going home, I was picked up by one of the studio chauffeurs, but when I grabbed the handle of the rear passenger door of the car it locked tight. The driver frantically tried to open it, but the central locking had malfunctioned (this happens regularly on my own car).

He was somewhat concerned as it was a brand new car. After a few minutes of tugging, he managed to open the door and we drove off at last in the direction of Euston station. Once more it would appear that my wayward telekinetic powers had disrupted things.

CASE 66 KICKING THE BUCKET

IN THE late 1980s, my friend Dennis Moyses and fellow members of the Ghost Club Society were taking part in an all-night investigation at a pub in Radcliffe on Trent, Nottinghamshire. Dennis told me that the pub had a reputation for being very badly haunted, especially the cellar. The landlord's dog refused to go down there and various people had seen things. Apparently, in the week before the Ghost Club investigation, the pub had even offered £400 to anyone brave enough to spend the night alone down there.

On the night in question, Dennis and a fellow club member drew the short straw and were to spend the night in the cellar. All was quiet except for the noisy droning of an ancient freezer until 3.30am, when there was an almighty clanging and banging noise. Dennis felt totally trapped and frightened as a bucket came flying down the stone cellar steps, their only exit. Both men, a little shaken, plucked up courage and made their escape back up the steps, keen to leave such a confined space. To their dismay, they discovered that the falling bucket was just a joke played out by the landlord, even though he assured them that it had been an accident.

It was quite an unnerving experience at the time, but it hasn't put Dennis off his avid ghost-hunting.

Unfortunately, on occasion, even in a building that is in all probability genuinely haunted, pranksters just can't help themselves.

ANIMAL
ENCOUNTERS

IT IS amazing just how often people whose homes I visit who purport to have a resident ghost also have pets who at times have acted like animal 'barometers', sensing sudden cold spots in a room, and seeing and reacting to all types of phenomena long before their owners do. Animals of all kinds have been said to react to imminent earthquakes in those countries of the world prone to tremors, when to most human eyes and ears even sensitive electronic equipment has picked up no clues or signs of change.

So, with perhaps this same, highly tuned set of sensitivities, they act as a sort of ghost sensor. Cats usually hiss and arch their backs in the presence of ghost activity, whereas dogs bark and howl and often slink from the room in terror. This can be true even if the ghost is one of their own kind.

Animal apparitions have regularly been seen and written about since man first picked up his pen. Stories abound of ghostly dogs and cats, and even the odd horse complete with rider. In Britain, there is a tradition of mystery black dog appearances (these could sometimes be linked to large cat sightings).

The size of the animal seems no bar to its reappearance after death. Cases on record in my files range from a small rodent to a Stone Age horse and rider. What follows are a few examples of this all-too-real group of hauntings.

CASE 67 THE HAMSTER

THIS NEXT case is amusing as it must involve one of the tiniest ghosts on record. The people concerned didn't tell anyone about their experience for a long time because they feared ridicule and disbelief. They told me I could report on it, however, if I protected their anonymity. To me the incident appears to be nothing more than a basic recording-type apparition. It is interesting, though, owing to the novelty of its subject.

The family concerned comes from the Northamptonshire village of Moulton, and consists of four sisters. They are all great animal lovers, and two of the sisters have often rescued abandoned pets and found them new homes. When they were young, the girls had a pet hamster, of which they were all extremely fond. When the hamster died (I believe most only live for about two years) they buried it in the garden, imagining that would be the last they would see of the small rodent.

However, one afternoon the sisters were watching television when two of them distinctly saw the long-deceased hamster scuttle across the lounge carpet and disappear behind a cupboard. Amazed, the girls both got up and looked behind the cupboard. They duly turned the room upside down, hoping to find the hamster, but they never did. It was nowhere to be seen. The two young girls both saw it and so the possibility that they were mistaken is small.

Telling me of the incident many years later, Tracey couldn't help but smile. 'You don't have to believe me, I know it sounds ridiculous. But what I'm telling you is the truth.'

The four sisters don't understand why, out of all the pets they have kept over the years, it was the hamster that chose to return. This may have been some type of recorded memory of the hamster in life, captured and re-triggered to appear at a much later date. If either sister had tried to touch the animal, they would have had an even greater shock, for their hands would have gone straight through it.

CASE 68 | THE DOG

IN 1996, the Hardy family spent the final couple of days of the school holidays camping at Holme in Norfolk. It had been extremely hot during their stay. Seeking somewhere cool, and something to do, they drifted aimlessly into what appeared to be a village hall of some sort, next to a little chapel. Their dog didn't like it, but they dragged him in anyway. It was icy cold inside and L could hear the distant sound of a child's voice. A woman's shout filled the air, followed by the sound of an organ being played. Those inside the hall heard thunder (it was later assumed that the sound was of the wooden chapel benches being pushed back to enable the children to sing). Then came the unforgettable first line of the chorus, 'All things bright and beautiful', followed by silence, a loud bang, and then nothing.

The strange spell was broken, and L dashed outside to where the rest of the family was gathered, because it had just been much too cold inside the hall. A tiny snippet of birdsong filled the almost unbearably warm air that day. However, the family couldn't help but look at the dog. His hair was literally standing on end and the poor beast was shivering uncontrollably, despite the intense heat. L Hardy wrote to me, interested to know whether anyone else had experienced something similar in that place.

I find two things in the story very significant: firstly, the dog felt the initial effects of the surroundings and became extremely unnerved by them; secondly, there was heavy weather at the time and a thunderstorm brewing. We have already seen how electromagnetic effects can influence paranormal experiences and sightings of apparitions. These may well also have a severe effect on the mood of dogs and other small domestic animals.

I believe that L Hardy stumbled upon a recording of that building's past. With the singing and other noises, this would fit. Maybe atmospheric weather conditions also played a part in enabling the activity to take place. I feel certain that they are not the only people to have been treated to a replay of the past in that village hall. It seems to me a classic example of the stone tape recording theory in action.

CASE 69 THE LITTLE SPANIEL

IT WAS on a hot summer's day in 1997 that Emma T had a strange experience during a visit to Ham House in Richmond. Ham House is Jacobean, with a history of ghostly activity spanning 200 years or more and reported by those who have lived in the house. Horace Walpole, in his writings of 1770, was the first to have put on record the spectral inhabitants of the elegant and beautiful house. These are said to include a small spaniel dog and the countess Dysart.

As Emma and her sister Sandra were visiting Ham House, they were particularly struck by the gorgeous painting of Lady Dysart in her sumptuous silken gown, cradling in her arms a small brown-and-white King Charles spaniel. With her auburn hair, the countess had a wistful, melancholy air about her and very sad eyes. Halfway up the stairs, the girls were met by a little dog. It was very friendly, said Sandra, 'jumping up on us and wagging his tail'. They told me that they were both surprised that the owners of the house allowed dogs free rein to wander, and he seemed to be on his own. They couldn't see a lead on him at all. Sandra pointed to a woman wearing red in front of them, and remarked to Emma upon her amazing likeness to an old schoolteacher whom they had both disliked intensely. When they came back down, the dog had vanished.

Emma told me that she suddenly felt her hands go very cold, as if she'd pushed them into a snowdrift. Shortly after this, the sisters departed and would probably have thought no more about it, except for a short article that Sandra saw by chance, on 26 February 1998, in the *Sunday Times*. Sandra couldn't believe it at first, and couldn't wait to show the piece to Emma. The article included a picture of Lady Dysart, the one that had caught their eye on the tour. It also documented the many ghosts both seen and heard at Ham.

These include the Lady herself, and her small companion, the spaniel, which is commonly seen at the bend on the stairs. The mystery, according to the writers of the article, may have been solved, at least in part. During recent building work undertaken in the orangery at Ham House, excavations uncovered the neatly laid out skeleton of a spaniel dog. Historians have worked out that, at the time of his burial in the seventeenth century, the orangery was part of the gardens. It would seem that this much-loved canine was laid to rest in front of the ornamental fountains. Such a place would only have been used for the burial of a dog of great importance. Mrs Graffius, who lives at Ham House, also believes that part of the mystery has been solved at last.

That evening after work, both of the girls read and re-read the article, and are now quite sure that they had both encountered the ghost of Lady Dysart's faithful companion. 'It would appear to fit with the facts,' said Sandra. 'The dog that we saw and stroked looked exactly like the one in the painting done centuries before. Also the weird coldness that I felt after seeing the animal and the fact that it was able to vanish like it did. We only averted our eyes for a matter of seconds, but maybe it broke the spell.'

The two sisters have told me that they intend to visit Ham House again soon. Who knows what they may see this time?

CASE 70 PUSSYCAT

BRIAN C and his wife Pat are a middle-aged couple living in Northampton. They are relief pub managers and had worked at numerous different public houses in the course of their careers.

Living in a new pub for a few short months made them question their previous scepticism on all aspects of the paranormal. There were so many odd occurrences during their stay in this particular pub, which had for a long time struggled to keep a permanent landlord. This was possibly due to the rough nature of the pub itself and many of the customers, as well as the invisible presence which was felt upstairs in the lounge, kitchen and bedroom.

Pat told me of bedcovers levitating and a mysterious figure seen walking across the bedroom in the night. The bed would move around at times, seemingly of its own volition. Most of the rooms were affected. Nearly every time Pat was at the kitchen sink washing up, she felt the sensation of fur rubbing up against her leg, like that of a cat when it wants to be fed. The first time this happened she thought it was their small dog; they didn't own a cat. But when she looked down, to her surprise nothing was there. No animal was ever seen at the time to account for this, and it happened continually.

Just before they left the pub, when the brewery had at last found a permanent landlord, Brian was woken up again by the bed being shaken violently by an unseen force.

Looking back, the couple found the many strange things that happened to them over the months during their tenancy hard to understand. They have never come across anything like it either before or since. The level-headed pair still almost refuse to believe in ghosts despite their many experiences of the phenomenon first hand (and told me that they wouldn't have believed it of anyone else). Also, they didn't want the name of the pub published for fear of upsetting any current or future tenants – just in case they were more fortunate and escaped such traumas (although Brian and Pat believe this to be unlikely).

CASE 71 THE PHANTOM DOG

KATE SNOWLING and her mother Valerie Faulkner were going out for a pub meal one evening in September 1997. They took with them Kate's one-year-old daughter, Chantelle. They chose to go to the Five Bells public house in the village of Bugbrooke, Northamptonshire.

Bugbrooke is a picturesque village with a particularly long recorded history. At one time, it consisted of a very large Quaker settlement. The village is cut in half by a meandering river. The Five Bells is directly opposite St Michael and All Angels Church, and is famous locally for its succulent steaks.

They sat down at a table and waited for their meal to arrive. Little Chantelle sat in a highchair at the table. She was at the stage of beginning to talk. It was Kate's birthday and both mother and daughter were busy chatting when Valerie noticed a black dog, a little bit like a sheepdog in size and shape, except for its colour. The friendly dog walked past their table with its tail wagging. Chantelle shouted out 'Dog, dog', or as near to it as she could manage.

Both her mother and grandmother kept dogs, and so 'dog' had been one of the baby's first words. The baby pointed excitedly at the animal and then it vanished. Mrs Faulkner told me that she didn't think for one moment that the dog wasn't real. The fact that Chantelle saw the dog too

The Five Bells public house in Bugbrooke, viewed from the church.

implies that there was definitely a dog of some description in the pub that evening. Kate told me that she didn't see anything. Indeed, if Valerie hadn't seen the dog vanish, she wouldn't have realized she had just seen a ghost.

The British Isles have a long tradition of phantom black dogs, from an enormous black creature famous in the West Country to ghostly black canines said to accompany lonely travellers on foot on the long trek home late at night. Many of these apparitions are thought to be almost demonic with blazing red eyes and frightening appearance. Sightings of phantom black dogs are much more prevalent in the vicinity of ley lines, which are thought to be channels of powerful natural earth energies. Most ancient churches are situated on these ley lines, and I find it significant that this sighting happened in a pub directly opposite a church.

This case goes to show that perhaps many of us have seen such a phantom without even realizing it, because of the dog's solid and ordinary appearance.

CASE 72 THE DAIRYMAID

WHEN I was 16, during the art college summer holidays, I worked for a few weeks with my good friend Heidi as a kennelmaid. The kennels were near Chertsey, Surrey, in a beautiful green and wooded area. They were family-run, and a friendly place to work. The work was hard, though, as it meant getting up very early and cleaning out rows of kennels, exercising the dogs and feeding them twice a day.

Heidi had her own accommodation, near to the owner's house and backing onto the woods. It was a small caravan, and for a time I shared it with her. The only problem with living in the caravan was that the toilet was on the other side of the field, not at all pleasant in the middle of a cold night.

It was good fun working at the kennels, apart from the occasional nasty-tempered dog. You had to go in and deal with them even if they longed to bite you. I remember a particularly scary and vicious dog, with a wall eye. His very appearance was enough to put you off. He looked every bit a thug. I was lucky, though, that none of the inmates decided to bite me; most of them seemed to love me, smothering me with sloppy kisses and jumping up for a hug. At the end of each day, I would be covered in hairs, mud and dog saliva.

Heidi told me one evening about the ghost that was said to haunt the kennels. Our small caravan was about 200 yards from the old farm dairy. It was sometimes used to house extra dogs if the kennels were full. There were about ten wire dog containers inside. It had never been my job to do the dogs in the old dairy, and so I hadn't been inside. My friend said that the place was badly haunted; some people had seen a female ghost, and any dogs put in the building quickly became disturbed.

Normally placid animals became aggressive, barking and howling non-stop. Others would become quiet and withdrawn, whimpering pathetically in the corner. As Heidi was telling me this, I could hear barking and howls coming from the dairy. I needed to go to the lavatory and as it was dark and very late it was quite spooky walking across the dark field to the small, brick, outside toilet block.

Next day, I was determined to see the old haunted dairy for myself, so I went there in my lunch break. It was a neglected, painted, brick building. Inside it was very cold, and the noise hit me when I entered. All the dogs, seeing a friendly face, obviously hoped for release, and shouted loud and long for attention. The atmosphere inside was horrible. In the air there was an almost palpable sense of sadness and decay. It felt as if it was haunted by someone who had led a terrible life and presumably had stayed on in part after death. One corner was especially bad. It is hard to describe, but it left me with a strong memory that I haven't forgotten even 20 years later.

As I went to leave, I noticed a tiny white dog, whimpering and partly hidden under his blanket. He poked his head out at me and wagged his tail. It was only a half-hearted wag, but it tore at my heartstrings. I opened the kennel door, and sat inside with him. I spent my lunchtime cuddling the animal and sharing my sandwiches with him. He didn't like being shut up in there any more than I would have done.

During the last few days, I visited the dairy every day. The dogs were always the same, behaving almost manically, but the little white one was pleased to see me. I left near the end of summer without seeing the ghost myself. I was disappointed, as I couldn't help but wonder what she looked like.

This incident reminds me of a story told to me by Reverend Bill Simons of Northampton. He said that many years ago at a local mental hospital, St Andrews, the staff noticed that one room was especially unpopular with patients, whatever their symptoms. Normally quiet patients sleeping in the room soon became psychotic and disturbed. This happened so often that it was remarked upon. In the end, the effects of the room were so bad that it was just used as a storeroom. As it is an expensive private hospital, this was a waste of resources.

Nurses were even frightened to go into the room to fetch supplies. Most of the staff speculated that the room was haunted, and there had once been a suicide in there. They eventually called in the services of a vicar and had the room officially blessed. All problems ceased, and once more the room could be used for patients.

73 SILKY

SUE PERKINS wrote to me to tell me of a series of incidents that occurred after the death of her cat. Mrs Perkins used to live in a Northamptonshire village, but has since moved to America. In July 1978, Sue came home from work one day to find her cat (who was named 'Silky', because of his lustrous soft black fur) dead at the side of the road. She buried him in the garden, and planted a yellow rose bush on the spot.

Roughly six months later, Sue was washing up at the kitchen sink when she noticed a little black cat playing in the garden near to the rose bush. It was so like her late pet that Sue quickly dried her hands and ran out into the back garden. By the time she got outside, the animal had gone. Sue decided maybe it had just been a coincidence and thought no more about it.

A few days later, she was sitting on the sofa watching a film on television. It was quite late and Sue felt drowsy. She was wondering whether to go up to bed or not, when she felt the familiar sensation of her beloved cat rubbing up against her legs. For a brief moment, she just thought it was her Silky; then, with some degree of shock, she realized it was not possible as he was dead. She looked down and could see no cat. It upset her, as she knew it was not just her imagination. Sue would perhaps have just dismissed the two incidents, if similar things hadn't continued to happen afterwards.

Over the next year, she told me, she must have seen Silky in the garden on a dozen or so occasions. He was frustratingly elusive, always being seen when she was in the kitchen and gone by the time she had run outside. This would occur late in the evening, usually when the weather was dull and damp (it sounds very much indicative of a recorded image).

On two or three separate occasions, too, the cat rubbed up against her when she was sitting on the sofa. Each time he was not seen, but only felt. After roughly 12 months, the visits stopped; although it was at about this time that Mrs Perkins got a new cat. Whether this fact has any significance, she finds it hard to be sure.

The whole affair has left her convinced of the survival of animals in some form after death. She feels that Silky sensed her sadness at his loss and returned to give her comfort. The apparition in the garden she feels was maybe just an image that became somehow frozen in time, that perhaps could only be replayed if atmospheric conditions, such as dampness, were favourable.

During my research, I have been told of many other cases of cats returning to visit their owners after death. The usual thing for them to do is rub up against the legs of their former companion.

GHOSTS AT WORK

INCIDENTS OF paranormal phenomena in the workplace are good from an investigative point of view, because there are usually many witnesses (ruling out hoaxers). The building where the action has taken place often has good records as to when it was built, previous owners and workers, and so on. Any deaths or fires on the site are often documented too. The same is not always true of a domestic dwelling, or at least such facts are not as easy to uncover.

Workers' reactions to a haunting vary. I have spoken to people traumatized after a frightening incident who felt they had to leave their jobs because of it, particularly when it is an ongoing situation. Others daren't speak publicly for fear of ridicule. Most work environments thrive on general leg-pulling and teasing, so it is quite understandable that many witnesses do not wish to talk about their experiences.

The exception to this is public houses, whose owners rightly welcome publicity, hoping that the fact that they lay claim to a ghost on the premises will attract the curious rather than turn customers away.

CASE
74 THE NEPHEW

THIS CASE is intriguing on two counts. Firstly, people appear to experience ghosts most often when their minds are distracted – in the sort of semi-aware state that we are all familiar with. This can happen when driving the car on a boring, familiar route taken every day, or even when just daydreaming while doing a repetitive job. The other significant factor in this story is that seeing the ghost was totally unexpected. The encounter should have had much more meaning, but on reflection seemed almost pointless. You should see what I mean by this after reading the story. I have changed the names of both of the characters concerned.

The incident occurred in a pub in the Northamptonshire village of Irchester. The village dates back centuries, and the high street bears testimony to this with its old sandstone buildings. William Underwood was in the pub one evening in November 1996. He was conducting a 'race night' there. This is an evening of pre-recorded racing films, chosen at random. Members of the audience can bet on the horses before each race begins and try to win more money than they lose. Such evenings are usually very light-hearted and fun, with the numerous horses given names chosen beforehand by the group.

Halfway through the evening Mr Underwood was changing the reel of film in the projector ready for the next race. The night was going very well and the atmosphere was jovial. A chef came out of the kitchen dressed in his 'whites' and walked past the projectionist. William Underwood heard him say 'Hello', and turned to reply. The young man said 'Hi, Uncle Will, all right then, mate'. William was surprised to see a familiar face and said, 'Hello'. He was unable to give the chef his full attention, owing to the fact that he was in the middle of changing the reel of film.

He told me with conviction that the man went in through the other door of the kitchen. Within a couple of minutes of their brief conversation, William went very cold. The man that he had just spoken to was dead, and had been for some time. Quickly he went into the pub kitchen looking for his nephew; there were others in there, but the tall, slim figure of his nephew was nowhere to be seen. None of the workers in the kitchen had seen him either, and, looking puzzled, told Mr Underwood that he was mistaken.

The young man concerned had died in a road accident months before. He had worked at that particular pub as a chef, and significantly his uncle remembers bumping into him there on occasion.

The whole incident upset and totally mystified him. Why would his nephew appear in this way? Mr Underwood wished so much that he had realized on seeing the young man the importance of the encounter. He could then perhaps have told him how much the family missed him, or maybe have taken a message from him to relay back to his family.

The thing that truly shook this man when I spoke to him, however, was the mundane reality of the whole experience – that is before he realized that the impossible had happened. I wondered at first if this could be an example of a recording-type haunting. This wouldn't appear to be the case, though, because in my experience interaction between the ghost and the witness can never occur.

Let me explain. If the ghost image is recorded in life by its surroundings and then the sequence is played back like a piece of video tape, it is no more real than that. We can't have a chat with a dead movie star while watching one of their films. The same is true of a recording. If Mr Underwood is correct, in some way he was able to see and speak to a person who no longer existed.

Could it have been a kind of time-slip – the two men having a brief conversation, but with the projectionist in the middle of a reversal of time, going back many months to the actual time when the young man was alive and working in the pub? There can be no easy or clear-cut answers to this question. Was it a mistake or an illusion? We shall never know. Perhaps one day, with the aid of scientific discovery, we will understand the mechanism behind such experiences.

CASE 75 WAKEFIELD POLTERGEIST

IN SPRING 1997, Gary Stock, a medium who specializes in performing the service of exorcism, was asked to go up to Wakefield in Yorkshire. Accompanying him was a television producer, Jurgh, and a film crew. They arrived at a warehouse used by the 'Imperial Car and Van Company', who had requested the help of an exorcist because many of the workers claimed that the warehouse was experiencing a poltergeist outbreak. As a result, their work had begun to suffer.

Nuts and bolts were being thrown around, hitting people on the head. No perpetrator was ever seen causing the trouble. While annoying for some, the activity had badly frightened others. Gary told me that when he first got to the building and walked in, he didn't sense any evil there, such as he was expecting, nor the unpleasant smell that often accompanies such hauntings.

Initially this led him to surmise that possibly the workers were mistaken and the place wasn't haunted at all, or that the whole thing had been caused by pranksters. However, as he explored the building further and climbed up the stairs, he rapidly changed his mind. Upstairs he sensed the presence of the spirits of two young children. Desperate to help resolve the situation, as he had travelled up to Yorkshire from London and for the first time was being filmed during his work, he concentrated and closed his eyes, trying to make contact with the children. After about five minutes, on opening his eyes, he saw the children, a boy and girl, and described them as follows.

The girl was aged about 10–12, and had long, blonde hair. The boy was younger. Gary heard the girl say the name Nancy over and over again, and understood this to be her own name. Gary asked her the name of the little boy, and she told him that it was Robert, her brother. She then said that over 200 years ago, long before the warehouse existed, they used to live nearby. Their father's name was Cooper, and he was a baker who owned his own shop.

They had always loved to play near the stream, and had been very happy, before both caught malaria (once prevalent in Britain) and died quickly. Somehow they were unable to move on from that place, and had become stuck there.

The medium then proceeded with the exorcism. He lit a lavender-scented incense stick and sprinkled some holy water around the warehouse, blessing the building. Then they waited for the atmosphere to change. He told the children that they couldn't stay, and they must move on into the light. As he finished the blessing, Gary saw two beautiful, blue, hazy lights that gradually faded until they were gone. With this the atmosphere of the place lifted from that of sadness to something more like normality. This was also noticed by the others.

Roughly four months later, Gary phoned the manager of the warehouse. He was interested to find out if he had been successful and, if not, whether there had been any further developments. He was glad to hear that since the visit there had been no more trouble. Everything was back to normal. Apparently, two others had tried before, without success, to rid the place of its ghosts. One was a vicar, the other a priest; so it seems to have been a case of 'third time lucky'.

The *Haunting at Wakefield* television programme, part of a series on the paranormal run in Germany, was shown to an audience of several million viewers, and provoked great interest.

CASE 76 THE BARRACKS

ROBERT SNOW is the editor of the Ghost Club Society magazine. The Ghost Club Society was set up in Victorian times as a vehicle for like-minded people from all professions to investigate the very real world of ghosts and to gather and collate evidence of all types of ghostly phenomena. The Society hosts regular all-night ghostwatches in haunted properties. Former eminent members have included Charles Dickens and Sir Arthur Conan Doyle.

Robert is now busy studying computers. His encounter happened many years ago, but may have gone some way to shaping his interest in the subject of ghosts. He was posted, in his army days, onto the permanent staff of REME School of Electronic Engineering, sited in Arborfield, Berkshire, and called the 'Hazelbrook Barracks'.

On the night in question, he was on guard duty and had to patrol, with a companion, the neighbouring 'Beaulieu' barracks, located about half a mile away. It was a disused barracks with lots of empty wooden huts on 'legs', known as 'spiders'. As Robert and his fellow soldier approached the centre of camp they saw someone walk towards them, then walk off between the 'legs' of one particular hut. The pair shone torches onto the figure, as they thought it was an intruder.

The moon was bright and so visibility was good. All of the security lights were on, too, so it would have been difficult to have mistaken seeing the man. The two soldiers ran towards the spot where he had disappeared and found no-one there. There was no apparent means of escape, as there was no available door into the building and all the windows were bolted and locked securely.

There had been many reports of strange happenings in that place; it seemed to have, in Robert's words, 'a rather unsavoury reputation'. Two hours later, the two men were walking along the edge of the parade-ground when they both heard the distinctive sound of someone marching briskly towards them. Yet, despite the fact that the whole area was well illuminated that night by all the perimeter lights, neither man could see anyone at all. The invisible feet passed within 20 yards of them and then the sound gradually faded away.

To the sceptic, Robert's experience could perhaps be written off as a mistake, or the hallucination of two tired and bored young soldiers on late-night duty. However, they were obviously not the first people to encounter weird goings-on at the barracks, hence its reputation. Robert tells me that he is very sure about what he saw that night. 'It was neither a mistake nor my imagination.'

CASE 77 | A HOTEL'S NON-PAYING GUEST

THE HOPCROFTS Holt Hotel is proud of its history, boasting that it is one of the most haunted inns in Oxfordshire. With many dramas and deaths over the centuries associated with the site, this could well be right! Perhaps the rather unusual and morbid decoration in the inn's entrance hall attracted ghosts and created a negative ambience: suspended from a large oak beam was a skeleton and an iron gibbet.

Outside the hotel, in the 1950s, a local woman reported seeing clearly the ghost of a cavalier. A young girl's bed was vibrated violently and she frequently levitated, in front of witnesses. When one considers the usual weight of a bed, this is quite a feat and seems to defy any known laws of physics. Other items of furniture were also moved and up-ended. This went on for months.

The account of the shaking bed puts me in mind of the now famous Enfield poltergeist case, investigated by Maurice Grosse and the Society for Psychical Research in the 1970s (see Case 97).

CASE 78 THE ELECTRA

THE ELECTRA cinema in Newport Pagnell, Buckinghamshire, no longer exists as a cinema. The building has been turned into a shopping mall, and changed beyond all recognition. In the building's original days as a cinema it was owned and run for many years by a sweet but eccentric old lady, Miss Salmons. She was tiny and silver-haired, with a love of wearing sandals all year round.

The cinema was, in its heyday, quite a grand, art-deco-style building, with a large entrance hall and seating on one level for several hundred cinema-goers. Upstairs was the living accommodation, on two floors, and a small private balcony with just a few seats.

As children, my sisters and I often sat on the balcony, watching Disney films, in the school holidays. For a time, both our parents worked there as projectionists. My mother eventually became great friends with Miss Salmons, despite the age gap.

Miss Salmons' father used to run the cinema, and it was his kind ghost that was said to haunt the place. Neither my mother nor my father experienced it, but many other workers there did. Apparently, while the projectionist was busy at his projector, he would sometimes feel a light tap and a hand on his shoulder. The old man had always done this when he was alive. It was one of his ways of seeing if everything was going all right in the projection room. Then he would fetch a cup of tea.

This room was always icy cold, and I remember as a child feeling it to be unusual, and wondering why. I did not like to be in there, especially on my own. Sometimes I would stand next to my father in that small room and peer through the little projection window, marvelling at the beam of light that made an image on the screen below us.

It was my father who told me of Mr Salmons' ghost. He believed in it himself. The only time that he had noticed that the cinema was haunted was in the 1970s when the film *The Exorcist* was being shown there. This was a controversial film showing the purportedly fact-based story of the possession of an American child, a young boy in reality but portrayed by a small girl in the dramatization. It showed the priest's attempts to exorcize the many demons. The film caused a sensation. Some people were so disturbed by it at the time that they were collapsing in cinemas, believing themselves to have become possessed, and all manner of jinxes were reported to have dogged the film's showing worldwide. I understand that the film has not been released on general video sale because of this.

Such was the case at the Electra. My father is not superstitious, and scoffs at anything supernatural unless he has seen it with his own eyes, but he said odd things happened during the showing of that particular film. For example, spools of film jumped from a shelf on their own and spun around on the projection room floor, and there were many other small, but creepy, incidents. Maybe the ghost of the former owner disapproved of such a film. Whatever caused the incidents, it was the only time such a series of events occurred.

My strongest memory of this lovely old cinema, though, will always be the individual Miss Salmons, with her mountains of collections of newspapers forming a sort of maze around her flat, her annoying black cat, and her occasional habit of putting her clothes on over her pyjamas, or vice versa, if she was in a rush. She was a lady who had known great riches in her youth (indeed she was one of the first British women to own and drive a sports car), but sadly she died with very little to her name.

LIFE-CHANGING EXPERIENCES

FOR AN experience to change your life, it surely has to change your *views* on life, either positively or negatively, and make you question previously held views and see the world in a new way. This obviously happens, for example, when a person survives a serious illness or a car accident. Other life-changing experiences might be the birth of a child, or an act of war.

It can happen with the death of a loved one, or after a profound shock to the system of any kind. As we become derailed from our own particular set of tramlines in life, we are thrown onto another, with different vistas. Sometimes this process forces us to become better people, more aware of the world around us, and consequently that of our neighbours.

The cases in this section are ones in which the experiencers and their subsequent lives changed maybe in only a small way.

CASE 79 | AFTER THE FUNERAL

SHEILA C lives in a picturesque village in Northamptonshire with her two children, and works in the medical profession. In 1997, her father died following a serious illness. Naturally all of his family missed him very much.

Some time after the funeral Sheila was woken up in the middle of the night. She instantly knew that there was someone else in the room, but was unafraid. In the half-light, she saw the familiar figure of her father standing in the room. He stood there for only a few moments, and then slowly faded away like a mist. He didn't speak, but she found his presence very comforting. This vision was totally unexpected, but welcome all the same. The next day she told her two children about it.

Such visits to the recently bereaved are extremely common in all cultures and parts of the world, and they tend to happen in the early days and weeks after the relative's death. Whether you argue that these visions are purely psychological in origin, or a good deal more 'real' in the sense that an actual presence of a spirit is in the room, is immaterial. These encounters are always beneficial to the bereaved and help them to come to terms with their loss more easily.

This story is very similar to the one about the artist Frank (Case 36), except that in that visit the lady's husband woke her up by calling out her name.

CASE 80 BLEAK HOUSE

ROBERT S considers himself fortunate in that in his life he has had some experiences that seem to defy rational explanation. Therefore one could well describe them as supernatural or paranormal.

His first such experience happened in the early 1960s. Robert and his family had moved to Southsea in Hampshire, as his father (who worked in banking) had transferred to Portsmouth with his job. Every Christmas the family would travel to nearby Dorset, to stay with friends who lived in a rambling old rectory affectionately nicknamed 'Bleak House', after Charles Dickens' famous novel.

When they visited Bleak House, they used to sleep in a room known as the sewing room. It was situated on a mezzanine floor halfway between the ground floor and the first floor. On one particular night, Christmas Eve or thereabouts, the young Robert had just finished reading and got up to turn out the light (there was no bedside lamp). He had nothing particular on his mind that night, and lay in bed with his eyes open watching the shadows play on the grey ceiling. The room was well illuminated by strong moonlight shining through the window, which overlooked the churchyard.

After a few minutes, he noticed a kind of circular, misty cloud forming over the end of his bed. It grew in size and emitted a powerful light. Watching the light growing in both power and density, Robert was astonished when it reached four or five feet across. He was at pains to explain to me that the mist seemed to be contained within a barrier. It seemed to be swirling about and getting thicker, yet at the same time it was confined as if in a glass globe. After a while, the young lad plucked up courage and jumped out of bed. He ran and turned on the light. The strange ghostly glow had gone. He sat on his bed for ages, very scared, yet too cold to remain out of his covers for long (the house had no central heating). Eventually deciding that he must have imagined the whole episode, he turned off the light and jumped quickly back into bed. Within minutes, the same thing happened again, but this time its size increased much more slowly. The boy felt almost compelled to watch the strange, phosphorescent glow. In the end, exhausted, he fell asleep, tiredness overcoming fear.

At breakfast next morning, Robert was mystified as to what he had seen in the old sewing room. He is sure today of only two things: firstly, that it was not his imagination or even a vivid dream; and secondly, that it was evil. The feeling around it was loathsome and impossible to forget.

This case reminds me of something similar I read about the keeper's house in the Tower of London. During a dinner party there one evening, a strange swirling mist was seen in the vicinity of the dinner table by all of the guests. That too was said to be confined within some type of invisible tube.

CASE 81 THE NECK AND THE CURSE

MRS THOMAS wrote to me because she was very distressed at some awful events in her life. These events were possibly paranormal in origin, and she hoped that I could shed some light on them.

The first of these was a photograph taken of her on holiday the year before. Mrs Thomas, her family and their two large boxer dogs had holidayed on the Isle of Wight. One day, they all went for a walk across some grassy land, reputed to have a history of witchcraft and pagan worship. Soon after the holiday, Mrs Thomas began to feel very unwell. She had severe stiffness in her neck and considerable pain. Her discomfort wasn't helped, either, when her holiday snaps came back, and on one of them, in the area of her neck, was a dark, coffin-shaped blemish, with white scratches across it. She showed me the picture, and I must admit that it had a very nasty feeling about it.

Her illness went on for months, and despite consulting specialists at various hospitals no cure was found. One doctor thought it could be a rare type of muscular paralysis. The dreadful photograph, with the neck erased, caused Mrs Thomas understandable disquiet. The case reminded me of a sort of voodoo curse, when an ill-fashioned doll is mutilated and the victim suffers a similar fate. Some locations seem to be almost powerhouses of negative energy, and I wondered if maybe the site on the Isle of Wight was such a location.

Mrs Thomas also felt that her house on the edge of Northampton was having a malevolent influence on her life. Feeling some sympathy for her, I promised to visit her house next day. I said I would be honest with my opinions, be they good or bad.

Waking up the next day, I was shocked to find that my neck was so stiff that I could barely move it. Thinking that maybe I had slept awkwardly the night before, I waited for the stiffness to pass. It didn't. Driving to Mrs Thomas' house was very difficult. I had to turn the whole of my upper body when looking left and right.

From the moment that I stepped inside the door of the spacious house, I felt a certain dread. Mrs Thomas explained that the 'off' rooms in her home were upstairs, so we went to investigate. The two rooms in question were the large bay-fronted ones facing the busy road. As I have found time and time again with haunted properties, the rooms were unnaturally cold. The larger room also seemed to be too dark. It was full of shadows, despite the large window.

However, of the two rooms the little boxroom next door was even worse. When I walked into it, I felt my breath to have been taken away. It was very difficult to breathe in there.

The two of us then went into Mrs Thomas' bedroom. The contrast was stark. It was warm, and had none of the atmosphere of the previous two rooms. Sitting on the bed, the middle-aged lady was flabbergasted when I told her I too had a stiff neck. I made a feeble joke that it must be catching (thankfully it was gone by the next day). She told me that since moving into the house she had developed asthma. I wasn't very surprised.

The previous owners had sold the property at a ridiculously low price. It would appear that they were desperate to move. When the keys were handed over, all they said to the new owners was, 'I hope you will be happier here than we were.' This was an innocent enough remark at the time, but Mrs Thomas can't help but wonder if they were referring to the nasty feeling of part of the house.

I suggested before leaving that if she was at all religious she might consider having the house exorcized. I believed the house to be haunted. It would seem wise to endeavour to do something to get rid of the awful atmosphere. On such a procedure I retain an open mind; in some cases it seems to work.

Other than that, there was a faint possibility that some kind of toxic substance in the small boxroom was causing constriction to the throat of anyone entering the bedroom. With regard to the unnaturally cold temperatures of the rooms, it was very odd. The house had central heating and didn't appear damp at all. I asked Mrs Thomas to contact me again with any further developments, and left it at that.

CASE 82 | PEBBLES FOR HIS GRAVE

IN MARCH 1998, after taking part in a television programme about ghosts, I got up to leave the studio. A grey-haired, friendly faced woman approached me. She commented on my necklace – a gold, star-of-David necklace that I always wear. It was souvenir of a lovely holiday in Israel, and an ancient form of protection.

The woman told me an interesting account of a visit to her husband's grave. She was surprised when she arrived there one afternoon to see the ground immediately in front of his headstone covered with small stones. She looked around, puzzled, for any children who might have placed them there while playing, but the cemetery was empty. On a whim, she counted the small, round stones. There was one for every year of his life. The woman told me that she felt the stones may have been placed there by paranormal means. If not, somebody, for whatever reason, had gone to the trouble of finding the correct amount and duly placing them in the spot.

There is a tradition among orthodox Jews at a funeral of placing a small stone each on the gravesite as a token of their visit, because stone is an eternal, longer-lasting than flowers or plants. This act has been immortalized in the moving and powerful film *Schindler's List*. At the end of the film, as the credits roll, all the chief actors make their way towards a grave arm in arm with the now elderly survivors from the real story and place stones on it.

CASE 83 A MOTHER'S VOICE

IN 1998 Debbie asked me to visit her house, not because she had a ghost (although in a way this turned out to be the case) but because she wanted me to do some palm-reading in her home. She had gathered together her cousin and various friends and neighbours. She lives on a 1970s housing estate on the edge of Northampton. It is not one of the best areas; the place is spoilt by a few vandals and the odd 'bad' family.

She had booked me about six to eight weeks earlier after hearing about me from a friend. I arrived at the house a little nervous, as I always am before doing any kind of psychic work. I never know how the evening will progress, or whether my powers will desert me in mid-sentence. This can happen on occasion. Sadly, I cannot turn my abilities on and off like a tap. I have very little control over them and feel grateful for the times when I am on good form.

Debbie had set up a table and two chairs in the small, homely kitchen. She made me a cup of tea and told me that some people had come for tarot readings and others for palm-reading. As I remember it now, I believe I saw seven people in all that night. I did Debbie first, and picked up quite a lot about her past, her young children and a terrible sadness that was surrounding her at that time due to a sudden death. At this point, she told me that she had only recently lost her mother, six weeks earlier in fact.

She told me that it happened only about a week after she had phoned me up to make the booking. She was thinking of cancelling the 'psychic evening', but her friends persuaded her to go ahead with it anyway, in case there was good news to cheer her up. After about 30 minutes, when I had finished Debbie's reading, I saw two other women who were neighbours. By now I was a bit tired, but I knew I still had much more work to do that evening. A young girl in her twenties then sat down at the table opposite me. She seemed a little shy, but she gave me her hand, eager to know more of the future. She had short, dark hair and glasses. The first thing that I picked up about her was that she was a student and very intelligent. She had a brilliant mind. Then, glancing up to look once more at her face, I noticed with shock a woman standing directly behind the girl, lightly resting her hands upon the back of the chair. She was smiling and obviously comfortable to be there. The lady was tall and slim and bore some resemblance facially to the sitter before me. Her clothes were unremarkable and she seemed very relaxed. She said to me, 'Give everyone my love. Please tell them I can speak now.'

With that she vanished, instantly. There was no gradual fade-out at all. It caused me to blink. I knew that for some reason I had just witnessed a ghost, a ghost with an apparent message, one that I didn't understand, but perhaps the girl sitting opposite me would.

I felt a little shy about repeating it, as it made no sense to me; but I did so, describing in detail my vision of the tall woman and her short speech. The girl went very white, and started to shake. I leant forward and held her hand, concerned that I'd upset her.

Then she explained. She told me, 'I am Debbie's cousin, the woman whose house we are in today. Nobody told you, but six weeks ago Debbie tragically lost her mum, my aunt. The woman you described. She had become ill suddenly months before with Motor Neurone Disease. It seemed to advance very rapidly in her case, she was still so young. Cruelly, near the end it took away her voice. So she couldn't speak and say goodbye to her family. She died so quickly. It must have been my aunt that you saw.' The girl then left the room, very moved, and I saw two others for readings that night, feeling slightly distracted, to say the least.

At the end, Debbie came up to me and thanked me for coming. She said that she was over the moon that I had seen her mother. It was wonderful how well she was and that she could now speak. Debbie also said that her little boy had told her that morning that he had seen his grandmother in the kitchen. Somehow the fact that I had seen her too just confirmed it all. I do so hope that she can now begin to heal after the death of her mother.

CASE 84 GOOSEBUMPS

THE FOLLOWING story is true, but even though I was there at the time I still find it incredible and hard to believe.

It was a wet and miserable day in late 1996. I happened to meet two very interesting people in a large café at Euston station. I have chosen to change their names owing to the sensitive nature of the case. One of them, Clive, runs a busy showbusiness agency and the other, Simon, is one of his clients, an actor/comedian. As we sat drinking coffee and chatting, Simon told me that a few weeks earlier he had seen an article, in one of his wife's women's magazines, about me. It was an article on electrohypersensitivity. As far as I can remember, it had been a bit silly and exaggerated, and so I was a little embarrassed when he mentioned it. Then, jokingly, Clive grabbed my hand to see if he would get a shock from it.

As he held my hand, I noticed his. (Among other things, I do palmreading, a skill I acquired so long ago I can't recall now how I learnt.) I always notice people's hands, and feel that the lines on them are like a map, exclusive to each individual, of our lives past and present. This is not, of course, set in stone, but there at birth as a guide to our potential. Sensing that Clive had a child, and that his wife was pregnant, I told him as much. He was taken aback. I gave him a few other details on his life, and said that his cousin Louise wanted very much for him to call.

Then Simon asked me if I could read his palm, even though he was a bit sceptical. His was more complex. I picked up that he had almost died once from suffocation (this had happened during his days as a North Sea diver), and that his child was ill but she would be all right. Amazed, he said that his baby daughter was in hospital, suspected of having a serious illness. He told me a few days later that she had improved and was at home.

Then I heard a voice, clear despite being a whisper. It was a man's voice, and it said, 'Please tell Clive not to drive his car. He could be killed today. I don't want him to get in his car. It's much too dangerous.' I knew it was a spirit voice, but I felt astonished nevertheless. I did not know what to say then. Could I be mistaken, or had I imagined it?

Somehow I felt that I must at least attempt to warn Clive about his car. So I blurted out, 'You're not going anywhere by car later today by any chance, are you? Because there's something very wrong with your car. Get rid of it.' Putting things gently has never been my strong point, and I did feel foolish, especially when the two men insisted Clive's car was fine, being quite new. Simon had a gig later on that day, and so the two had to travel down to Brighton. They had no choice.

However, a bit freaked by the accuracy of my other information about them, they reassured me that they would have the vehicle checked over at the nearest garage. We said goodbye, promised to keep in touch, and went our separate ways.

Next lunchtime, I received a phone call from an excited showbiz agent. Apparently the pair went to the nearest garage after our meeting, not thinking for one moment that my information could be correct, but just to make sure. The mechanic checked the car over and told them it was lethal: the brakes were faulty, and there was a 6-inch nail through one of the front tyres which would probably have resulted in a blow-out, not a good prospect on a busy motorway.

Clive told me over and over how grateful he was, as he believed that I saved his and Simon's lives that day. Then he asked how in the world did I know about his car, when he hadn't suspected a thing. So I told him of the whisperer. There followed a rather stunned and palpable silence. He said that his good friend Tony had died in a car crash months before. We both realized together that it had been Tony's voice. I know it gave him goosebumps. It did me.

About two weeks later, I was in London again, and so I dropped in at the agency to see how they were getting on after their near escape. Walking into the small building near to the railway bridge, I sensed at once that it was haunted. It was being haunted by Tony, and his presence was mostly in the back room corner by the coffee machine.

I informed Clive of my suspicions; a young secretary overheard our conversation. She went white. The woman too had felt a coldness and presence next to the drinks machine and was a little afraid. Hoping to confirm the identity of the ghost, and as a kind of test, Clive said, 'See if you can pick out my friend from these photos.' There were six. I think the other five were of his clients. One I recognized as he was actually a famous soap actor.

One photo seemed to leap out at me, however, and so I chose it. It was correct. I believe now that I was meant to meet those two men that day, if for nothing other than to warn them of the hidden danger they both faced. Perhaps the dead man had tried to contact his friend but couldn't make himself heard. His kind spirit could not bear the thought of Clive facing the same awful fate.

THE COSMIC JOKER

HERE ARE some odd stories – some are amusing, and others the complete opposite. They prove that anything can happen, and frequently does. At times it appears that the so-called 'cosmic joker' is at work, causing chaos, coincidence and bizarre events.

CASE 85 A BAD HOUSE

CERTAIN HOUSES appear almost to attract ghosts, or at any rate types of powerful psychic energy. There is evidence that the ground a building stands upon can generate some of this energy.

In 1921, Hereford brewer Alfred Watkins noticed, while out riding one day on a local hilltop, that through the modern cultivated patterns on the land he could make out a web of lines linking ancient sites and churches. For a long time, he investigated this and concluded that these were power lines (known as ley lines) of the earth known by ancient man and tapped into. Numerous books have been written on this subject. At the junction of these lines, nodes are formed, and it is supposed that here the power is most concentrated.

Most churches, standing stones and sites of significance are thought to be built on these leys. Running water, whether under or above ground, is also commonly a factor in places of paranormal sightings. It does perhaps create its own field of energy. These two energy sources could have played some part in causing the peculiar happenings in the last house where I lived.

It was a picturesque, seventeenth-century cottage in Bugbrooke, Northamptonshire, fronted by the river Nene. For the seven years that my family lived there, all manner of unusual incidents took place. In part, they generated my interest in this field of research, and in a way pushed me into writing about others' experiences of ghosts. The first ghost that I saw, in the garden, was that of an elderly woman. As our

The author's former home in the village of Bugbrooke. This was the scene of some major paranormal event.

house had a particularly large garden with lawns, fruit trees, and beds, I struggled to manage it, and so advertised in the local village shop for a gardener. A week after this, driving up to the cottage, I noticed a woman of about 60 standing by the gate. She glanced at me and then turned and walked off into the back garden. I quickly got out of the car, thinking that the lady must have come enquiring after the gardening job.

I was cross that she'd gone into the garden without asking me first or waiting to speak. When I went through the wooden gate and looked for my bad-mannered visitor, she had disappeared. It was only then that I realized that the woman in the brown, tweed skirt and sensible shoes was dead. It was the lady who had lived in my cottage about a year earlier, and had since died of cancer.

It was a vivid and real sighting, but I didn't understand. Why had she come back? What was her purpose, and why had she disappeared when I followed her?

For a few days I told no-one, but in the end, wanting to talk about my experience, I asked my husband Paul if perhaps he had seen the old woman. He hadn't, and I could tell that he doubted me. Eventually, to my relief, we found a real flesh-and-blood gardener, but it wasn't too long before the mysterious happened again.

My last child Becky had justed started school. In a way, it was nice that the house was quiet for once. She had been at school for about a week; it was mid-morning and I was standing in the lounge tackling a huge pile of ironing. From upstairs in one of the children's rooms came the sound of children talking and laughing accompanied by the noise of marbles being rolled along wooden floorboards (the room was carpeted). Thinking that it must have been the radio on in the other room, I went in to check. The radio wasn't on, and the noises continued, steadily getting louder.

I climbed the stairs, really puzzled now. At first, I wondered if my two youngest children had sneaked home from school and were playing upstairs. When I opened the door and entered the bedroom, all noises halted abruptly. The room was still but there was a different atmosphere, like when small children have been naughty and a parent enters the room. Somehow the atmosphere of mischief hangs in the air, palpable and strong. I checked every inch of the room and all the cupboards. There were no children in there. I never heard the playful, happy, ghost children again.

The two other strange incidents occurred about two years later. It was early morning and I was making my children some hot porridge for breakfast. The green melamine bowls were set out ready on the worksurface. As I went to pour the porridge into one of the bowls, Becky screamed, 'Mummy, mummy, the bowl just moved.' I had seen it move too, but still half asleep I hadn't believed my eyes.

I poured some of the porridge into the bowl, but it slid several more inches away from us. Laurie and Becky both started laughing, saying it was 'magic', and commanding (like stage magicians) 'Move, bowl, move.' I put my hand out to grab the bowl, and it smoothly slid along again, quite quickly as if by some invisible force. In all, before it stopped, the small green bowl had moved three or four feet.

We all supposed that perhaps the worktop was wet and that the warm porridge had caused the object to constrict, propelling it across the smooth surface. This wasn't the case, however, as the worktop was dry, and it wasn't on a slope. The three of us were stunned and at a total loss as to an explanation.

Other peculiar incidents in the kitchen involved the cutlery. First of all, we would go to the drawer only to find items bent and misshapen: usually forks, and normally just one prong. It was near impossible to straighten them up, and despite the fact that it was a very expensive set of heavy stainless steel (thankfully not the best family silver) we had to throw many pieces away. It is very hard to eat comfortably with a bent fork, without cutting your mouth. Not to be left out, the teaspoons also started to develop a kink at the joint of the handle and the bowl, and always in the same place.

This annoying distortion of the cutlery went through a very active phase for a few months. After almost every meal, the fork that I had used would bend, sometimes while I watched.

Many other people were witness to this, including a young radio researcher who visited the house in 1997 to interview me about the problem. She seemed quite a sceptic at first, but her views soon changed. I held up a fork to show her how it had bent previously, and it suddenly drooped and wilted like a flower until it was completely misshapen. The girl was amazed, and said, 'Oh my god.' She was recording the interview at the time.

The last incident that I remember well occurred when Paul and I were sitting one evening watching one of *The Omen* series of films. We were both engrossed in the scene where the catholic priest runs into the church clutching the baby Damien – the anti-Christ – to his chest. In this part of the film, all hell breaks loose, with the icons covering the walls of the church falling dramatically to the floor and smashing.

The author with some of the many electrical and household items she has affected over recent years, owing to supposed 'electrosensitivity'.

As I watched the film, sitting curled up in my big favourite arm-chair, I shuddered, thinking the scene awful and quite frightening. Suddenly the large oil painting of a French landscape with cattle literally leapt off the wall, hitting me on the head. For a horrible moment, what was being played out on the screen became almost real. Because the picture was glass-fronted, it hurt a lot. Both Paul and myself were astonished and I made him switch the television off.

Inspecting the picture cord, Paul was surprised to see it was still intact, as was the sturdy nail that had attached it to the wall. I have no idea what made that picture behave in that way, but I tentatively speculate that it may have been telekinesis, or mind-over-matter. Maybe, without realizing it, I was so disturbed by the film that in some way mind energy replicated the action in the film, causing it to happen for real in my living room. This is, of course, speculation.

Many other paranormal-type events occurred in our house over the years, too many to remember. A German film crew came to document some of the more spectacular activity. In the end, I became used to living in a house that seemed to be haunted.

Today I believe that I sometimes caused some of the activity inadvertently by telekinesis. This was very annoying and disruptive at times, as I had (and still have) no control over this. There seemed to me as well no possible earthly use for these new-found unusual powers. Ruined cutlery cannot be used, and to have objects leap off the wall and hit you on the head is no fun at all.

Despite all this, the house wasn't bad. In fact it was completely the opposite, cosy and attractive with beautiful views and a garden that always looked green and colourful whatever the season. It was fronted by the river and overlooked the cricket ground. I miss it still.

Living there gave me a good grounding in what happens during a haunting. In fact, many of the events were poltergeist-like in nature. Now, when I visit ordinary people in their homes, I usually know what questions to ask, and more importantly what clues to look out for. It is often hard to talk about these things, as most people simply disbelieve anyway. It takes a strange sort of bravery to come out in the open about it all.

86 THE SLEEPING BAG

DENNIS MOYSES is an energetic stalwart of the Ghost Club Society, and somebody who I am glad to consider a friend. He once told me the following amusing story. It was during an all-night ghostwatch vigil, in Suffolk, in a church reputed to be badly haunted. The leader of the small group was Mr P, and the incident took place in 1994.

I have been on an interesting ghostwatch with Dennis myself, in 1996 at a pub called the Queens Arms, in Essex, so I am familiar with the unusual equipment that he takes with him on such occasions. Apart from the obvious camera, in case of being lucky enough to spot an apparition, he also takes his folding garden seat, a flask with a hot drink, and if the venue is cold (a castle, church or deserted graveyard) he has even been known to take his sleeping bag along too. As he said to me, 'I'm not getting any younger, and my old bones don't appreciate the cold any more.'

Dennis told me that when the group arrived at the church at the start of the evening, Mr P said, 'Whatever happens tonight, don't panic.' They all laughed at this, of course, not imagining for one moment that any of them would panic. Then the group chose their places in the empty building to settle down for the night.

After about an hour of near silence, there suddenly came the loud and unmistakable sound of the heavy church door slowly opening. The large, circular, black, iron door handle turned, and inch by inch the thick oak door opened.

At this, the formerly brave leader leapt to his feet and scurried to the back of the church, afraid. His action scared Dennis, who told me he finds it hard to be brave in the face of others' fear. What made it worse was that they could see, now the door was fully open, that no-one was standing behind it; only a blast of cold air swept in from the graveyard.

Jumping up too, Dennis attempted to get as far away from the door as possible, forgetting in his haste that his legs were snugly confined in his sleeping bag. He ended up in an undignified heap on the church floor. All escape was quite impossible. By the time he was free of his constraints, all fear had left him, and laughing at the ridiculousness of the situation he got up and closed the door.

Nothing else unusual was to happen that night, except for a possible small gift left by the forgetful 'ghost'. As the group left the church at the end of the vigil, Dennis noticed on a small table on the right-hand side of the porch an old-fashioned gentleman's cap. A cap wearer himself, he was certain that the table had been empty upon their arrival. None of the other members present that night professed to owning the cap, or having seen it before. It didn't belong to any of them. Those present that night couldn't help but wonder if the sudden appearance of the cap and the earlier dramatic opening of the church door were connected in some way. Overall, it was an amusing evening and one they have never forgotten.

CASE 87 RAT-A-TAT-TAT

AN ELDERLY lady, Patricia C, wrote to tell me of her strange experience. Patricia lives in the centre of Northampton in a very ordinary house. Shortly after the sudden death of her husband, she heard knocking sounds. It always happened at night when she was in her bed getting ready for sleep. The knocking seemed to come from the wooden headboard of the bed. It was quite loud, as if someone was hitting the wood with some degree of force.

Naturally, Mrs C was very puzzled and scared. She tried moving her bed, and placed it against the far wall; but still the knocking sound could be heard. There were several hard raps, then silence. She became distressed, finding it hard to sleep. She thought it could be connected with her husband's death, but was at a loss as to what to do about it.

In desperation, she told her local vicar about it. He came round to the house and blessed the building. Eventually, the knocking ceased, and Patricia put the whole incident behind her. However, she can't help wondering if the noises were some kind of attempt by her late husband to contact her.

This type of phenomenon is extremely common following a death. I have had other similar cases reported to me. One was from a woman following the death of her aunt. This time the knocks seemed to originate from a wardrobe. This was short-lived, just as in Patricia C's case. Another case I heard about involved loud banging noises from the attic following a family bereavement.

CASE 88 | STRANGE PHENOMENA AT SOUTH LODGE

MAZDA M told me about the strange occurrences she encountered when she lived at the beautiful old South Lodge, Blair Dalrey in Scotland, from 1983 to 1996. The house dates back to 1650. Additions were made to the building at later dates. It is an old gatehouse and has no nearby neighbours, being bordered on three sides by woodland. It has a pretty rose garden and latticed windows, making it the perfect retreat for Mazda and her husband, who are artists.

Almost as soon as they had moved in, the haunting began. This was to include many aspects. The first things they noticed were ghost dogs, seen as something like a blur at first but later more clearly. They were moving about at speed, giving the impression of being very excited. Mazda described them as like an unfocused image or something photographed at speed. These friendly dogs became regular visitors and were even felt brushing against the couple's legs.

They were to find out later that a previous owner had kept three red spaniels at the lodge years ago. Mazda was unafraid of them, as she imagined them to be 'images recorded in the old stone walls and activated during certain weather conditions' (they were only ever seen during cold damp weather). Open fires provided the sole form of heating in the cottage but some rooms proved impossible to heat, the kitchen in particular. Mazda took up dowsing as a hobby, and found that there was possibly an underground stream running beneath her home.

Later on, the voices began. This frightened the couple, because the voices would wake them in the middle of the night. The voices sounded like people talking on the radio. The source was never located and remains a mystery.

Many other mysterious events were witnessed by the couple when they lived in this particularly haunted cottage, such as apparitions, orange balls of light, and teleportation of small household objects. These phenomena were also witnessed by friends. Mazda's husband developed postviral syndrome and became quite ill for a time, having to give up work. The couple even closed their design studio. Mazda's husband felt somehow that the house was draining his energies.

They decided to move; for a while things got worse, and so they asked a spiritualist medium to cleanse the house. She told them that the house was haunted by a woman named Margaret from the late eighteenth century. She had lived there with her blacksmith husband and four children. Margaret had died suddenly in the kitchen (this was later confirmed). The medium achieved some success in cleansing the house of its negativity, and the temperature in the rooms also improved. The couple, however, still moved out as planned three months later.

CASE 89 GENTLEMAN OF THE ROAD

ALTHOUGH THIS incident happened over ten years ago, Emma has never forgotten it. She can find no easy explanation for her very fleeting experience and believes others to have seen the same thing. Emma was in her thirties, and worked on evening shifts. She was driving home late one night, as was entirely usual, along a stretch of fairly quiet country road, near to Bedford where she lived. She had had a good evening's work, and received decent tips, so she was in good spirits, although feeling a little tired.

Towards the end of her long journey she saw a man illuminated in the car's powerful headlights. The man was some distance ahead, but, suicidally, walking in the middle of the road. Wondering how best to avoid a collision with the strange man, Emma sounded her horn, loudly but to no avail. The man was either deaf or stupid.

As she drove up closer, the young woman saw his clothes in detail. He was wearing a very large, grey coat that almost brushed the floor and brown leather boots, and he had a messy wisp of corn-coloured hair. He looked dirty, and was obviously a tramp, a man of the road, seemingly untroubled by the nuisance of traffic.

The young woman had to swerve to avoid hitting the 'tramp'. As she passed him, she saw his face clearly; it was brown and ruddy, with many missing teeth and a friendly countenance. Breathing a sigh of relief, Emma drove on, but she took a quick backward glance at the old tramp. He had vanished without a trace. There were no high hedgerows or ditches for him to have fallen in, or even any trees to hide behind. Emma shuddered, somehow knowing that she had just seen a ghost, maybe condemned to wander the roads, fields and hedgerows forever, as he had done in life.

He sounds very much like a recording, and recordings are coincidently often seen in and on the location of roads, hence the large amount reported each year by stunned motorists. I honestly think such apparitions could be responsible for unexplained car accidents. A driver, seeing the entity, swerves to avoid it, and hits the undoubted metallic reality of another speeding car instead. Such roadside visions are common and almost a part of British culture. Probably the most famous example is the Bluebell Hill ghost (Case 99).

90 SPARKY

JEANETTE S was bored, waiting on the corner of St Edmunds Road, Northampton, on St Valentine's day. It was starting to get dark and had began to rain softly. She glanced into a nearby shop window to pass the time. Jeanette saw her reflection in the glass and couldn't understand just what she saw there. All around her, and seemingly being emitted from her own body, were hundreds of tiny, red sparks. The sparks covered her entire body.

Jeanette spun around quickly, thinking at first that some prankster was training some sort of laser light device – the type that lecturers use to point to an area on a lecture screen at a distance – on her, from a car perhaps. The cars were all passing at speed and there appeared to be no-one nearby who could have done this.

She turned back to look again, thinking she had been mistaken or imagined it all. The sparks were still flying out from her body. A few minutes later, walking away from the shop in the direction that her friend was expected, she noticed that the phenomenon had stopped. Seeing her friend up ahead, young Jeanette babbled out her strange story to an initially disbelieving ear.

This soon changed. Later on, as the two passed the cemetery, Jeanette's friend Jill screamed out; for, in the semi-darkness of the Northampton street, she could clearly see and feel tiny, red sparks jumping erratically from Jeanette's body and hitting her on the chest. The two girls were terrified and ran all the way back home. Both were concerned that their clothes could catch on fire. These weird effects had ceased once again when they reached home.

When Jeanette told me of her strange experience years later she was still puzzled as to the cause. She told me that at the time she was suffering with exceedingly painful periods. On the evening in question, it was the first day of her period. She wondered if the red sparks were linked to this in any way. Could they have been an odd externally visible response to the pain she was feeling? It was impossible to say, but if this was not the result of some bizarre hallucination felt and seen by the two girls, then the cause is yet to be determined.

I told Jeanette that the incident put me in mind of two quite separate areas of the paranormal: Kirlian photography and the field of SHC (spontaneous human combustion). Over the last few decades much has been written about both, but for the benefit of those unfamiliar with them here is a brief outline.

Kirlian photography was discovered by accident in 1939 by a Russian engineer. The man had put his hand too close to a live electrode, receiving a shock. This was accompanied by a spark of light not unlike that of light in a tube where neon is charged electrically. He decided to experiment to see if he could photograph this reaction. He used two metal plates, acting as electrodes, and placed photographic film on one of them. He carefully placed a hand between them, and his wife switched on the current.

When the film was developed, it showed a distinct kind of spreading, glowing aura being emitted from his fingertips. Other objects were then photographed using the same method. They all, even leaves, emitted sparks. Even stranger, when a leaf was cut in half, a weak light was emitted around the missing portion of the leaf. The 'auras' were of a different colour and density, depending on the subject photographed.

This was quickly hailed by some enthusiasts as evidence of the aura of light, which all humans possess around them, that could be viewed by some mediums and psychics. It is often described as a corolla of light. This could well be the origin of the halo painted on religious icons, and said to denote purity.

Proponents of this unusual type of photography said that by studying pictures of individuals it was possible to see evidence of and diagnose diseases, such as cancer. This is as yet unproven.

Many interesting books have been written about SHC, especially in the last ten years. This phenomenon is reported even now all over the world. These mysterious fires are said by witnesses to burn the body from inside out. The process is very rapid, and starts with sparks or a bluish flame being emitted from the victim prior to the inferno to follow.

One of the more famous cases concerns a young girl at catering college who burst into flames in front of her horrified fellow pupils. The girl did not die immediately from her severe injuries, but in hospital a few days later when her lungs failed. Witnesses spoke of a blue flame on her shoulder as she walked along the corridor.

This process was famously touched upon by Dickens in *Bleak House*; an elderly gentleman in the book suffered this fate. Dickens, who was an accurate chronicler of the times in which he lived, was believed to have been inspired to write of this rare cause of death by an account he read in a newspaper.

Victims are found reduced to a collection of charred ashes with only the bony extremities, such as the feet and skull, escaping the ferocity of the fire. These victims more often than not are elderly people living alone, so there are no witnesses and no-one to extinguish the flames. When found later by the emergency services, these deaths have sometimes been written off as the results of a carelessly discarded cigarette or a fall into the fireplace of the victim, the fat in the body (it has been argued) acting as fuel and the clothes as a sort of external wick. Thus, it is argued, the unfortunate person has become a human candle.

Other researchers in this field argue, quite rightly in my view, that, as the human body is composed of more than two-thirds water, this would prove almost impossible. Water is not usually regarded as highly combustible. They link the phenomenon with a high incidence of sunspot activity, microwave radiation, and a bizarre sort of internal rapid cellular degeneration, when cell mitochondria break down and create a rapid chain reaction, a bit like that of a nuclear explosion. This causes the water in the body to heat up and separate into its components of hydrogen and oxygen, adding fuel to the fire, quite literally. A good read for those interested in this subject is *Fire From Heaven*, by Thomas Harrison.

CAUGHT ON FILM

THE FOLLOWING section is quite short, indicating the rarity of instances when an apparition has been caught on camera, be it a still camera or a video camera. With the advent of photography came some really obvious fakes. Genuine pictures are in very short supply. I have only ever come across a handful that showed any potential of being evidence of the paranormal. Most look simply like double exposures, the work of faulty cameras, or poor developing of the pictures themselves.

CASE 91 THE VIDEO ENHANCEMENT

WHILE CARRYING out some research in 1996, I appealed through the media for witnesses to the paranormal. I received something very interesting in the post in response. It was a video recording of an ordinary riding lesson taken a decade before by Martin Emmott. Martin's daughter was having a lesson at Cobham Manor Riding School in Maidstone, Kent.

It was late afternoon a few days later, when Martin was abroad on business, that his wife and daughter decided to watch the video. They noticed an odd figure standing at the edge of the riding area in a position where it would be impossible to stand owing to the dense hedge and undergrowth. No extra spectators had been noticed by anyone at the time of the lesson.

The film was shown to the owner of the riding school. He had suspected that the school could be haunted, as his horses often spooked for no apparent reason. Wanting to find out more, he sent the film off to a nearby television studio and they put it through a type of enhancement process. This appeared to confirm that the apparition did have a Pilgrim Fathers' type of appearance and attire. His face was so thin as to appear almost skeletal, and he had a mass of what looked like coarse, grey hair. His clothes were dark but there was some sort of ruff or neckerchief at his throat. The figure appeared to rise out of the ground, but was unfortunately only visible for a matter of seconds. The sequence of film is now quite worn, owing to the wear and tear of over a decade of viewing. Incidentally, the strip of land that runs along the back of the riding school is called 'Pilgrims Way'.

Some months after writing up this short story and publishing, with Mr Emmott's permission, a still of the footage, I was approached by the popular *Fortean TV* programme on Britain's Channel 4. They wanted an unusual story and had heard about my work gathering evidence of the bizarre. I judged that the riding school story would make for good television. It made an interesting piece, with the rare exception of having some accompanying evidence, however small. *Fortean TV* sent me, as a 'thank you', a copy of the episode with the ghost at the riding school. It was good to be able to see the footage after it had been sharpened up by the TV crew. It looked a lot clearer than when I had watched it months before at home on my video-recorder. I believe this to be one of the few cases in the world of a 'stone tape ghost' caught on video. Perhaps the apparition, in his lifetime, stood one day, or regularly did so, on that spot at the side of Pilgrims Way, and somehow by a process as yet little understood his actions appear to be frozen in time like a fossil in the rock or a footprint in concrete.

With the increasing use of video cameras by more and more families, such occurrences should in theory become far less of a rarity. To the sceptics, of course, video footage can be faked just like photographs; it is actually far harder to do this with video, however, and it certainly was ten years ago.

CASE 92 A TAP AT THE WINDOW

OCCASIONALLY PEOPLE who suspect that their home may be haunted catch evidence of it on camera while simply taking an ordinary family snapshot. Kate S and her husband and baby daughter moved into and renovated an eighteenth-century sandstone and brick cottage in the village of Walgrave, Northamptonshire. The renovation work needed on the house proved to be quite extensive, but when the couple had finished the work it became an attractive and bright home with oak beams and an open fireplace.

They suspected their new home had a cellar that had been boarded up for some reason. Part of the quarry-tiled hall floor sounded hollow, and when they opened up the understairs cupboard door they felt a draught. However, as they didn't relish the thought of all the work and mess needed to uncover the cellar, they left it alone.

Kate had a feeling that the house could be haunted, but wasn't too concerned, even when her husband was on night shift and she and the baby were on their own. One day she was in the kitchen working when she heard someone knocking at the window. The kitchen window overlooked the small back garden. Worried about a possible intruder in the garden, she looked outside. The garden was empty and it didn't look as if a bird had flown against the glass. This would be unlikely, as the window is on a side extension with a high stone wall almost directly in front of it. The garden gate was also locked to prevent the dog from escaping.

At about this time, she received some photographs back from the developers. All the pictures in the reel of film came out entirely normally except for one of the baby in her baby-walker in the lounge. In front of the baby, and being observed by the dog, is a mist-like shape. Kate couldn't help but ponder if she had accidently caught a ghost on camera, despite having not seen anything unusual at the time.

It is ironic, but in most cases if someone sees an apparition and tries to photograph it they seldom have any success. However, when apparitions are occasionally photographed nothing is seen by the person at the moment they take the picture.

CASE 93 | PUB PROMOTION

THE GREY-HAIRED and bearded Peter Coles is a retired engineer. He has had a succession of interesting jobs, including 15 years spent at the BBC in a variety of roles. He is also a keen amateur photographer, having taken pictures since the age of 11 when he lived in the north of England.

His 'local' is now the Kings Arms public house in the town of Newport Pagnell, Buckinghamshire. It is situated near to a river, and is a few hundred yards from the former Electra cinema (see Case 78). The pub is a large brick building recently refurbished and given a smart exterior coat of white paint. Not far from the pub, in what is now called Priory Street, was Tickford Abbey. The pub and some of the surrounding houses are situated on what would have originally been part of the monastery grounds. The land was swallowed up gradually as the town grew in size from the original small settlement.

In February 1995, the then landlord (there have been two more since), an Australian named Graham, asked his friend Peter for a favour. Knowing him to be an amateur photographer with some talent, he asked whether Peter could take a few shots of the bar, and in particular the large new menu board above it. The photos could then be used as publicity in all the local papers to advertise the fact that the Kings Arms was changing and expanding its menu.

Graham had always been interested in good cuisine, and to show off the new range of food on offer had commissioned a colourful new menu board from a local signwriter. He had made a good job of this, and the result hung above the bar with illustrations and descriptions of the fare on offer. It was painted onto a blackboard so as to look as if it had been chalked up. Peter laughed when he told me that the only thing that was actually chalked up was the prices.

Peter agreed to help his friend out, and promised to come round the next day, just before opening time, to take some pictures. It was about 11am when he set up his equipment as promised, but as it was a dull February morning the light in the pub was very poor. The photographer suggested shooting a practice run of film and having another bash at it following day. He shot the roll of film, but despite the use of a photography umbrella and flash the results were quite poor, as he had expected.

The next morning they tried again. This time it was a bit later, and an elderly regular, Ted, aged 76, was in the pub with his German Shepherd dog, Lazer. Ted came in every day for a tipple. He usually had only one drink, and always sat on the stool at the left-hand end of the bar. He tended to bring along his dog for company, so Graham, who also kept a German Shepherd, would shut his own dog out at the back to avoid any fighting between the two. On the morning in question Lazer would not sit still. This was unusual, as he was normally very obedient. The dog kept looking into the right-hand corner of the pub, growling loudly and barking. Then he stalked along the front of the bar, crouching down low as if afraid of something.

Ted remarked that he couldn't understand what had scared the animal; he had never been like it before. So, after finishing his drink, he said goodbye and set off towards home. None of the three men had seen anything strange in the room to account for the behaviour of Lazer.

Peter, using film of a faster speed and a different camera for this second attempt, began taking some pictures. He told the landlord, who posed behind the bar, to stand very still while he took them, because if he moved at all they could come out blurred. He was hoping this time for success, as Graham was in a hurry to have the pictures ready in time for the introduction of the new menu. In order to get a good angle for his shots, Peter stood in the doorway of the adjacent room (this no longer exists, as the wall was recently knocked down to enlarge the bar area). He shot the second roll of film. In the interest of speed, instead of developing the prints himself, as was usual, he took them to a local developer for an express service.

Later on, the two men viewed the prints. The first few looked good, and they were pleased: success at last. Halfway through the stack of prints there was a run of seven. What they saw in these surprised them so much that it took their breath away. In the right-hand corner of all seven photos stood the figure of a monk. He could be seen clearly, but was not as sharply in focus as Graham. The monk looked to be quite small in stature, and was dressed in a faded brown habit, with a kind of bluish rope belt tied around his waist. His head was bowed slightly forward, and so his face could not be seen. It was covered by his hood. In his hand, there appeared to be a walking stick. Some of the pictures showed the figure in far more detail than others, and he seemed to be moving forward and fading out of focus.

Peter told me that the image must have been in his camera's view for maybe two or three minutes, as despite the rapid speed of the film he had paused between shots for a few moments. The two friends realized at once that they had inadvertently captured this unseen ghost on film, especially considering the earlier, strange behaviour of Lazer. It would seem to be the case that the dog was able to see the monk, even if no-one else could.

The men presumed that, because of the close proximity of the Kings Arms to the location of the former Tickford Abbey, their ghost was one of the monks who used to live there. It was puzzling because, to Graham's knowledge, no-one had ever before reported seeing the figure of a monk in the building.

The pub did lay claim to having two other ghosts that have quite often been seen and heard over the years. They are said to be a phantom pianist and a bowler-hatted gentleman who on occasion has been seen sitting at the bar by customers and staff alike. Those who have seen this smartly dressed gentleman think he is from about the 1920s era. They have even initially taken him to be a customer and so his appearance must therefore be fairly solid and lifelike.

Word soon got round the small town about the apparition of the monk and the picture appeared in the local papers and a publication issued by the brewery. Peter told me that one of the British tabloid newspapers offered him a great deal of money for the seven negatives in 1995; when he refused to sell, they tried to steal them. As he did not particularly need the money, and rather liked the negatives, he decided wisely to keep them.

Locals wanting a copy of this unusual photograph swamped him, asking for copies. He told me that he must have printed up dozens of these over the following months, even producing some poster-sized prints. These were pinned up all around the bar area and remained there for months. The ghost had become quite a talking point. He gave one of these pictures to a Mrs Sharpe who kindly passed it on to me in 1996, knowing it would be of interest.

I believe the picture to be a very rare example, and I can't stress enough exactly how rare, of an apparition of the recording type. It shows a snippet of Newport Pagnell's past history: the monk slowly traversing the monastery gardens. Although the scenery has changed dramatically in the ensuing passage of time, the actions of the monk have remained totally unchanged.

I suspect that, as is normally the case with such recordings, the images are very gradually fading out, so much so that they are now invisible to the human eye. This may not have been true of these images perhaps 200–300 years ago. Then the monk apparition could well have looked three-dimensional and sharp, so that anyone witnessing him on his travels would have taken him to have been a living person instead of a ghost.

The other two ghosts mentioned earlier could also simply be stone tape recordings. They are clearer than the monk because they are a good deal more modern in origin. The environment in and around the pub could well meet all of the criteria that are necessary in order to create and hold these images. Perhaps the Kings Arms is built on top of some of the rocks used in the earlier construction of the monastery and its surrounding walls.

The building is also situated very near to the river, and hence running water. In so many of the cases of this type that I've investigated the phenomenon occurs near to or directly above a source of rapidly flowing water. As yet, I have no firm ideas as to why this factor can influence the capturing of images – the most common form of haunting – so positively. I hope one day soon to find some answers to this question and in so doing solve another part of the mystery of ghosts.

Since the pictures were taken, there have been two other landlords, and the bar, as seen in the photograph, has changed virtually beyond recognition. A wall has been knocked down and the room completely redecorated. The bar now runs along what was the right-hand side wall in the photograph taken by Peter. If you visited the pub today, the position in the room where the apparition appeared is roughly where the 'Specials' blackboard stands and next to the spirit optics behind the newly positioned bar.

I hope to visit this pub with Peter Cole and, using exactly the same camera film and flash gun (so as to replicate the original conditions as closely as possible), attempt to get some more photographs. If my theory is correct, maybe we will be able to capture this ancient apparition on film once again.

FAMOUS HISTORICAL CASES

THIS FINAL section comprises a few of my favourite classic cases. Looking at these years, even decades, later, one gets a new perspective on them. Whether you can believe them or not, they are all landmarks in the history of ghostly activity and how the world's media report on it. These stories will probably still be told well into the next generation and beyond.

CASE 94 | MYSTERIES AT BORLEY

THE FIRST case is the Borley Rectory haunting made famous particularly by the flamboyant, self-styled ghost-hunter Harry Price in his writings about the house and its grounds. He investigated it extensively over many years.

Borley lies two miles from the market town of Sudbury in Suffolk, near to the river Stour; its nearest neighbour is the village of Long Melford. Even though the rectory no longer exists (it was destroyed totally in a fire years ago) it still attracts sightseers and tourists. Even as the big house was burning down, some said that they saw mysterious figures at the windows as the flames danced.

A lone, ghostly nun has been reported to walk in the gardens in the direction of the church, along what has been named 'The Nun's Walk'. The church is also supposed to be haunted. Indeed, the whole area is rich in the tradition of ghost stories and legend, and has a romantic history with its own coach and headless horses.

The rectory was built in the late nineteenth century and was described sarcastically at the time by one observer as an 'ugly red-brick monstrosity'. It was built to house the Reverend Bull and his 14 children. The house was large by any standards, and downstairs its rooms included a library, a scullery, a sewing room, and numerous other rooms. From the available pictures that we have of the house, it has a solemn and depressing look about it. It is not attractive, like many other buildings of the period. It was built purely for function and not beauty.

The long legend of Borley Rectory started with the Reverend Bull and his family. The children claimed to see apparitions, such as a death coach, in the grounds, and all manner of strange phenomena. This became common knowledge locally. Later, due to the construction of an extra wing on the house, it became an almost hollow square in shape. Such a shape led to high levels of noise on windy days which could have been ascribed to ghosts. For more details, see Robert Wood's excellent book *The Widow of Borley*.

I know about the unusual sound effects that the weather can cause with some old buildings. In the last cottage where I lived the back porch, a later addition to the house, had a few loose tiles on the roof. When it was especially windy, the wind would get beneath the tiles, producing a whistling noise that sounded almost human. Indeed the first time my mother heard it, she asked who was whistling.

The rectory was also associated with a suspicious death, that of Harry Bull. His sisters put it down as murder, but this was never actually substantiated.

However, the couple who made the haunting the world-famous drama it was to become were Reverend Algernon Foyster and his young bride Marianne. Both were eccentric in their own ways, which led to a joint instability. He was a physically decaying old man, when he lived at the rectory from 1930 to 1935, and his mind was suffering too. His wife was a vivacious, attention-seeking, strikingly attractive woman, whose husband (it was rumoured) couldn't satisfy her sexually. This became apparent when she later installed a young lover in the house, with the tacit approval of the rector himself.

The haunting soon developed from the rather benign apparitions seen by the Bull children into a spiteful poltergeist, who scrawled nasty messages on walls and moved objects at all hours of the day and night, creating mayhem. Some of these scrawls have been captured in photographs taken at the time. Throughout the long duration of the haunting, Reverend Foyster scribbled busily away on a book all about his home and the unusual happenings in it, hoping to become a famous writer himself. Those who saw his ramblings knew this to be a false hope. The haunting was interesting to many, the *ménage à trois* surprising to most, but the vicar's manuscript was disappointing.

The phenomena at the rectory were investigated by Harry Price and members of the Society for Psychical Research and a séance was held there. Recorded activity in the history of the poltergeist outbreak included eerie lights and noises, bells ringing, water turning to ink, and the movement of objects and furniture. The couple left Borley after five years, under a cloud of rumour, suspicion and hearsay.

Marianne spent the rest of her life moving from place to place, ending up in America. The vicar died a slow death after leaving his famous address, arthritic and worn out. More recently, the couple's unusual marriage and personalities have attracted as much interest and attention from writers as the ghosts themselves. The whole story is like an onion, with so many layers that, however many truths or lies are stripped away, you can never really get to the bottom of it. Whatever was behind the haunting, I believe it was nothing like the dramatic portrayal projected to the world by Marianne and subsequently the media. She perhaps used the situation as a way of spicing up her boring rural life, living with an elderly man in the middle of nowhere with little prospect of excitement and a house that was a dinosaur – an ugly relic of the bad taste of another era, and hard to run without an army of servants and plenty of money for its upkeep. It was a house originally built for a family of 16.

The ghost stories were not started up by the couple, but subsequently they ascribed all sorts of probable natural phenomena, such as the acoustics of the place, to ghostly activity. Buildings do seem to absorb emotions, and a part of the personalities of those who have lived in them, creating a record of former inhabitants, not just in the decorations and furnishings used but within the very bricks and mortar.

This particular house is a case in point. It is a building of unusual construction that seemed never to have been loved, with a succession of eccentric owners, situated in a remote and melancholy spot. The whole thing is a recipe for a haunting. We shall of course never know how much of it is truth or fiction. The only ghost one can now hope to see there is the lone nun walking in the gardens. She is perhaps the only genuine one there anyway.

I have yet to go to Borley, but hope to visit the site soon. I don't expect to see any apparitions there, but I shall take my camera just in case. Once again, natural forces could well have been at work here. The church and rectory might well be on a ley line. Many people believe these invisible lines of energy can enable images and sounds to be stored and played back later, although the existence of this ley energy has yet to be proven conclusively. Lots of researchers have studied these leys and strongly consider that they can trigger the sightings of ghosts.

Famous cases such as this have given Britain the tradition of being the most haunted country in the world, with more ghosts to the square mile than anywhere else. This is almost impossible to measure but is useful for attracting tourism. I believe that Britain's long, varied and at times extremely bloody history is the reason for its high predominance of ghosts and legends.

CASE 95 THE BRONZE-AGE HORSEMAN

THE FOLLOWING is a classic case that has already been fairly well documented. It has even been televised in the form of a dramatic reconstruction. However, I am fortunate in that one of the original witnesses wrote down comprehensive notes immediately afterwards; these I can quote from directly, as I have been given them by his grandson Robert Snow.

> In 1924 I was in charge of the excavations carried out by the Society of Antiquities on the late Bronze Age Urnfield at Pokesdown near Bournemouth, Dorset. Every afternoon I drove down to the site and returned at dusk. One evening I was motoring home along the straight road which cuts between Cranborne and Sixpenny Handley. I reached the spot between the small clump of beech trees on the east, Squirrels Corner pinewood on the west, where the road dips before rising to

cross the Roman road from Badbury rings to Old Sarum. I saw away to my right a horseman travelling on the downland towards Sixpenny Handley; that is to say, he was going in the same direction as I was going. Suddenly he turned his horse's head and galloped as if to reach the road ahead of me and cut me off. I thought he was just a stable lad, from the racing stables two miles further back along the road.

I was so interested that I changed gear to slow down so that we should meet, and so that I should see who the man was. However, before I had drawn level with him, he turned his horse again to the north and galloped along parallel to the road and about fifty yards from it. I could see that he was no ordinary horseman, for he had bare legs and wore a long, loose coat. His horse had a long mane and tail, but I could see neither bridle nor stirrup. His face was turned towards me, but I was unable to see his features. He seemed to be threatening me with some implement, which he waved above his head in his right hand.

I now realized that he was a prehistoric man, and did my best to identify the weapon so that I could date him. After travelling alongside my car for about 200 yards the rider and horse suddenly vanished. I noted the spot and found next day, when I drove along the road in bright daylight, that the spot coincided with a low round barrow close to the side of the road. I had never noticed it before.

Many times afterwards, all hours of day, when I was weary or alert, I tried again to see my horseman. I tried to find some bush or other object which my tired brain might have transformed into a horseman, but with no success. I made some enquiries in the district, and after a few months Mr Young, the well-known iron craftsman of Ebbesbourne Wake, told me that he had asked many of his friends at Sixpenny Handley if anyone had ever seen a ghost on the downs between the village and Cranborne, and that at last an old shepherd, George Raymond of Gussage and formerly Alvediston, had asked 'Do you mean the man on the horse that comes out of the opening in the woods called Squirrels Corner?'

A year or two later a friend of mine, Mr Alexander Keiller, a well-known archaeologist, wrote to me as follows. 'Your horseman has turned up again. Two girls, daughters of Harry

Foyle of Oakey Farm, Handley, cycling from Cranborne one night for a dance, complained to the police that a man on a horse had followed them over the downs and frightened them.' Mrs Young, wife of James Young, told me recently that she was at the family tea party when her husband mentioned to those seated at the table what Mr Keiller had said in his letter to me. The daughters of Harry Foyle, being cousins, were of the party, and said they were the girls mentioned in the letter, but had not mentioned it before for fear of ridicule.

Captain B. Cunnington, the curator of Devizes museum, had told me that his grandfather and Colt Hoare had opened the barrow and found in it the bones of a man and his horse.

Mrs Young and her son recently told me the account which old shepherd Raymond gave to Mr James Young, as follows. Shepherd Raymond used to feed his sheep on Handley Downs every day. He took his dinner with him in a red handkerchief. When he had finished his dinner he always smoked his pipe. One day he had finished his dinner and was sitting on a bank near Squirrels Corner. He saw as he was filling his pipe a man on horseback come out of the green lane between the trees on his right. He did not recognize the horseman. Finding to his dismay that he had no matches in his pocket, he hesitated, and then got up and walked towards the man, who had turned his horse towards him to ask for a light. Just as he approached the horseman, both horse and man vanished.

At the beginning of the twentieth century, it was a tradition in the neighbourhood of Handley that the ghost of the wicked Earl of Shaftesbury haunted Handley Downs on horseback. (This would have been the 1st Earl of Shaftesbury 1621–83). What is special about this case, if it is a recording, is the sheer longevity of it. If the primary witness is correct in his assumption of the man's era being that of the Bronze Age, he must be one of the oldest apparitions recorded.

CASE 96 AMITYVILLE MADNESS

THIS NEXT classic case, one I first read about when in my early teens, will be familiar to many people. It occurred in the mid-1970s at the address of 112 Ocean Avenue, Amityville, New York, USA. I can well remember reading it with a mixture of horror, disbelief and eagerness to reach the next page. It was the stuff of nightmares, and at the time I cared little for the truth (if there was any in those pages), since it was such a good story in itself.

Here is a brief outline of the basics of the case, now over 20 years old. The first part is definitely true, as it is based on the police arrest and trial records. Ronald Defeo, a young man previously of good character, went berserk one night. It was 13 November 1974. He walked around the house in the middle of the night, and shot dead his entire family as they lay in their beds asleep. The last to be killed was his sister. There was no earthly reason for his actions. In those hours of darkness, the young Ronald Defeo was a man possessed.

Roughly 12 months later, George and Kathy Lutz moved into the Defeos' old house, with their three children. The large, attractive, Dutch colonial-style building was incredibly cheap at $80,000, probably due to its bloody history. Almost from the moment that they moved in, the family of five claimed to have endured a haunting so terrifying that within weeks they were to flee their new home, reduced to emotional wrecks.

The whole incident is captured in the bestselling book by Jay Anson. Phenomena occurred in most of the rooms of the house, as well as in the garden and boathouse. Green slime oozed from the taps and black slime from the walls. Plagues of smelly flies bred in the house (probably attracted by the slime). A mysterious hooded figure was seen and the small daughter began talking to an entity invisible to everyone but herself. Cloven hoofprints were discovered in the garden, and the face of a pig was seen at an upstairs window. This form was thought to be demonic.

Then, disturbingly, the master of the house, young George, began acting strangely. He grew a beard, and started to believe he was possessed by the killer Ronald Defeo. Work became impossible for him and he suffered a kind of mental breakdown. Anyone living in such a house could be forgiven for going slightly crazy, I feel, if any of the claims about it are actually true.

Hastily to the rescue came Father Ralph Pecararo, who on entering the property heard an evil voice telling him to depart. He sprinkled around liberal quantities of holy water, to little apparent effect. Then the family discovered a small, hidden room under the stairs, painted in blood red. (Indeed it could even have been painted with the aid of blood. I read of a certain castle where blood was mixed with the paint to achieve the desired shade.) The use of this oppressive room could not be guessed at, but it seemed tainted by a bad atmosphere.

In mid-January the Lutz family fled the house, fearing for their sanity. They left in absolute terror in the night, never to return. Their story became an overnight sensation. Films were made of it as well as the best-selling book. Apparently, even the manuscript of this book was said to have become jinxed by the evil surrounding this case. It was nearly lost forever in a car crash. Actors on the set of the film suffered from accidents and ill health while filming the events. The original house was not used in the filming as it was said that no-one was able to stand the atmosphere in there.

The people who now live in the house without any trouble feel the whole episode to have been a fraud, perpetrated by those out to make money. They even attempted to sue the Lutz family because they were pestered by camera-wielding sightseers for months. Eventually the sceptics took the story to pieces and the Lutz family retracted a lot of their former testimony.

The author of the book had never actually met the priest who blessed the house, and he based his accounts on tapes lent to him by the clergyman. The author, himself a sufferer of poor health, was said never to have actually visited the house, which was ironically called 'High Hopes'. He based most of his book on hearsay, second-hand testimony and his own excellent ability to spin a yarn, which cannot be underestimated as it made him a lot of money.

Looking back now at this old case, is there anything to be learned from it for ghost-hunters today? I think there is. It shows just how powerful the human imagination can be, especially when it is coupled with the runaway-train effect of an excited press and media when they have got the scent of a good story. I believe that much that happened in that house defies an easy explanation, not least the murders. To annihilate your whole family takes a total breakdown of the self, for in wiping out your own family you are in a way destroying a large part of yourself by destroying the gene pool that would go on into the future. No-one will probably ever know why that young man chose to commit such an act.

He did indeed seem possessed by a great evil, something that was later on to be attributed to the house, but I consider that argument to be flawed.

It was only because of the awful acts committed there that the unfortunate house took on its malevolent connotations. They left behind a sort of negative psychic imprint. Added to this, because of the high media attention covering the killings, any future inhabitants of 'High Hopes' would be fully aware of its grim past. Surely this factor alone would severely colour one's opinion of the place. Any strange noises, leaks of water in the building, or mood swings suffered by those living there would take on a greater significance than they would normally.

Maybe the house was haunted. It is impossible to tell now. It seems unlikely, but of course one can never rule it out. The whole fantastic episode is an excellent demonstration of the sheer scope and power of the human imagination. When confronted with evil, our minds often conjure up greater and greater horrors. However, the greatest horror of all in this story is its beginning – the mass killing of an innocent family. This alone is more frightening than anything dreamt up later and turned into book and film.

CASE 97 ENFIELD ENIGMA

THE CASE of the Enfield poltergeist is famous the world over. It was widely reported by much of the world's press and captured in the excellent book by a favourite writer of mine on the paranormal, Guy Lyon-Playfair, entitled *This House is Haunted*. I can remember first hearing about it as a young child and being fascinated. I must have been around the same age as the child in the case, Janet (a pseudonym), and so I felt a particular interest.

For those few of you unfamiliar with the story, and even for those who know it well, I shall briefly describe it. It started in the council house of a single-parent family, named Harper, in London in late 1977. It began, as many cases of its type do, with unexplained noises and movements of objects and furniture. Mrs Harper was afraid and confused by the whole episode from the beginning and called in friends and neighbours. They witnessed some of the activities, which tended to centre around the lively 12-year-old Janet, a girl at that difficult time in a child's life, the onset of puberty.

Very soon, the local and national press got to hear of the haunting, and two reporters from the *Daily Mirror* went there and kept vigil, witnessing (it is claimed) a chair fly unaided across a room. The family were to know little peace and normality for many months, not just because of the haunting but also due to the intrusion of assorted researchers who visited the house. Most had the best of intentions, but did not want to miss out on a slice of the action, and action there was aplenty.

The long list of activities included whole rooms of furniture either upended or moved, beds violently vibrated and shaken, bedclothes repeatedly pulled off by an invisible hand, levitations of young Janet, footsteps, the sighting of two apparitions, and the failure of electronic equipment brought in by researchers. A lot of the effects happened in the girl's bedroom, a room shared by Janet and her sister. This room was made famous by the series of photographs of objects supposedly being flung through the air. In the photos, there is a look of elation rather than fear on Janet's face. The pictures are easy to date, as there is a large poster of actor and singer David Soul on the far wall, in his role in the series *Starsky and Hutch*, so much a part of teenagers' TV viewing in the 1970s, and many a girl's heartthrob at the time. The girl was also seen to levitate, by a neighbour while walking along the street, clearly through the bedroom window.

She would enter trance-like states, and eventually a deep, guttural voice, more like a growl, was heard emanating from her. This has been recorded on tape and is almost as famous as the photographs. It is disturbing to hear. The evil-sounding voice made numerous claims as to its identity. One of them was said to be that of an elderly man who lived in the house before the Harpers. The voice is almost too deep and masculine for the fragile-looking Janet to have made, although of course one cannot rule this out, however unlikely. It appears as if a bizarre energy force is using her throat to manifest itself and be heard, presumably in the absence of a usable throat of its own (making distinct similarities with the case of the Bell Witch; see Case 98).

The case was thoroughly researched by the Society for Psychical Research and in particular Maurice Grosse, who obtained much evidence of paranormal activity over the months. Despite the fact that some of it was obviously caused deliberately by the children on occasion to perpetuate the attention (all children crave attention), I believe the haunting to be genuine and therefore very important.

A relative named John spent a lot of time with the besieged family, and for his troubles had various objects thrown at him, including in one instance Janet herself, knocking off his glasses. He appeared on a television programme in 1998 with Maurice Grosse, Albert Budden, and other researchers on the subject. He struck me as a genuine and sincere person.

Despite Janet being the apparent focus of the haunting, her mother appears to have suffered the most from the very public ordeal played out in front of an eager press. She looks terribly strained in any of the photographs that feature her. She seems totally bemused by all the attention on her home, which would have been uninteresting to anyone before the weird events of 1977.

Two reporters from the Society for Psychical Research visiting the house declared it all to be trickery, and said that they had seen no genuine activity during their presence. Added to this, the 12-year-old girl was caught on video camera bouncing on the bed, to look like levitation, and bending with force cutlery and metal bars. In spite of this blip, it is fairly certain that unusual things did occur with regularity at Enfield. Witnesses included visiting police, neighbours, relatives and researchers. The drama lasted from August 1977 to September 1978.

I recently read in a women's magazine that the long-suffering Mrs Harper still resides at the same London address and has bravely remained there despite all that has happened and the fact that the building must be full of bad and disturbing memories. She has lost her son to cancer, and a daughter has also suffered from a form of the disease. Now elderly, in the years following the outbreak Mrs Harper has endured bad health herself. All this would hint at an indication of possible environmental factors operating in the house and its vicinity. These could be anything ranging from radon gas (common in Britain) to high local electromagnetic fields, chemical or gas pollution, or even slight seismic activity. Such environmental factors have recently been implicated in hauntings and also as a cause of long-term disease, both serious and chronic (see Case 61).

This is a strong probability in this case, which fulfils the three classic criteria for this sort of phenomenon:

1   a family group that includes a pubescent or pre-pubescent child;

2   a family suffering poverty and disharmony at the time;

3   a council home (statistically these have a higher probability of experiencing a poltergeist outbreak).

This last fact has been used as an argument by sceptics, claiming it to be a ploy by council tenants trying to effect a move or house-swap if they are unhappy, for whatever reason, with their accommodation. This could well be true of some, but is not the case with the Harper family, as the mother continues to live at the same address over 20 years later. If her intention was a swift move to another premises, she has been spectacularly unsuccessful.

The events at Enfield are interesting to me on three specific counts: psychologically, parapsychologically, and historically. If one places it squarely at the door of the power of the human mind to conjure up images and hallucinations, then it was an example of hallucination on a massive scale that sucked in and fooled many members of the population; either that, or Mrs Harper and her children were veritable magicians, producing some effects worthy of their being made honourary members of the Magic Circle. From a parapsychology standpoint, the episode ran the whole gamut of poltergeist effects ever reported, and because of its longevity was able to be rigorously tested by the resident experts at leisure. This is rarely true in other instances, and is what makes this case stand out from the rest. Lastly, from a purely historical human viewpoint, the case is a true landmark in the long history of hauntings, a history that is as common to humble dwellings as to magnificent stately homes or crumbling castles. This fact is often brushed aside by the numerous writers of fiction concerning ghosts.

CASE 98 THE BELL WITCH

THE STORY of the Bell Witch has gone down in history as possibly one of the most malevolent poltergeist hauntings ever recorded. It seemed to go on for ever and encompassed a vast range of phenomena. In the two years of its duration no family member escaped torment.

The episode occurred in the early 1800s to a prosperous farming family, the Bells. They were Baptists by faith. The focus for most of the more spectacular aspects of the activity has been quoted as Betsy or Lucy, depending on which source one reads. Both were only young girls at the time. It doesn't really matter to this story which girl was initially the focus, as in the end most of the activity seemed to concentrate on the unfortunate Mr Bell.

It started when the farmer saw a strange, large, black dog in one of his fields. Like any farmer would, he took at shot at the creature. This was to be the end of normality for the Bells. From then on, if we are to believe the reports, there was little peace in that particular household. Various family members, especially the girls, would be slapped hard around the face by an invisible hand. Moaning and gasping noises were heard, like someone trying desperately to speak. As is the case with hauntings of this type, many of the neighbours were to witness some of the vast range of phenomena which included unexplained lights, falls of stones, and even one of the girls vomiting copious amounts of pins, on more than one occasion.

Eventually, this malevolent poltergeist was to find a voice, telling with some relish various accounts of its origins. According to the voice, it was buried in the local woods, its grave had been disturbed, it was the spirit of a local woman and even that it had been around for millions of years. The voice added that because of this the family would never be rid of it. A black maid employed by the family, and previously thought to have been happy there, was hounded with cruel insults. She was slapped and spat on, so much so that on one occasion her hair became quite wet. She was particularly disliked for some reason.

Then the focus became John Bell himself. The farmer developed a strange, undiagnosed illness. He found it increasingly difficult to eat and swallow. His tongue swelled up to uncomfortable proportions. The poor man slowly worsened and he got sicker. He was worn down by the unremitting chaos in his home that was to last for almost two years, and close to breaking point. Just before Christmas, in 1820, he died. Rumour has it that he was poisoned and that his medicine had been laced with something lethally toxic (the cat swallowed some and promptly died). Of all of the unfortunate Bell family, he seems to have suffered the most assaults and those with the greatest ferocity.

Bedclothes were regularly pulled from the beds in the night, and scratches at the window kept the family awake. However, as always seems to be the pattern in hauntings of this type, the phenomena gradually lost momentum. This was particularly noted after the death of the head of the family, John Bell, and when several of the older children left the farm and lived elsewhere. Eventually the whole thing completely died down, despite the poltergeist's threat to return in 1935. It never did and the farm in the end changed hands.

This story seems to incorporate virtually every type of paranormal phenomenon. The long list includes disembodied voices, the sound of flapping wings, physical assaults, and disruption of items of furniture in the house. The episode culminated in the death of Mr Bell. This is what makes the story so disturbing. Not only did the Bells have to put up with two years of utter disruption, but they probably lost their father as a direct result of all the stress.

Sceptics could argue that the story is an exaggeration, or untrue, or that the farmer's death was purely accidental. They may be right, but as hauntings go if there is indeed some truth in the fantastic saga of the Bell Witch, then it must be what any paranormal investigator would call 'a worst-possible-case scenario'. Thankfully, it never normally gets quite as bad as this.

CASE 99 THE BELLE OF BLUEBELL HILL

THE BRITISH Isles have many cases of roadside ghosts, and sightings often go back many years. My own county of Northamptonshire has several. These include phantom carriages and horsemen. There have even been reports of a phantom motorcyclist. Some of these stories can be quite unnerving, especially the incidents when a driver picks up a passenger, usually along a lonely stretch of road late at night, only to find their passenger disappears suddenly without a trace without opening the car door. Some of these unfortunate motorists have reported such incidents to the police.

My favourite case in this category is the famous phantom of Bluebell Hill, near Maidstone in Kent. Many motorists over the last few decades have reported either seeing this ghost or colliding with her. A taxi driver, Maurice Goodenough, once ran over the girl at about midnight. He described her as about ten, and wearing white socks, a blouse and a skirt. After stopping his vehicle, Maurice Goodenough wrapped the girl in a blanket. He carefully placed her on the path and quickly went to get help. When he returned, the accident victim had simply disappeared. No trace of her was found; even police with tracker dogs failed to find the girl. There was no trace of blood on the road, either, as one would expect after an accident.

Others have seen the girl and tried to give her a lift, only to see her disappear. The local police have had numerous reports from shocked motorists. The ghost is said to be a young girl killed on that stretch of road in November 1965. She was on her way back home after a fitting for a bridesmaid dress.

Other witnesses have described seeing a phantom girl who appears to be much older than the girl encountered by Mr Goodenough. It is extremely unlikely that there are two ghosts haunting this particular stretch of road; therefore, either people are mistaken in guessing the height, age and general appearance of the same girl, or only some of the witnesses are telling the truth. Personally I favour the second explanation. When a location becomes well known as a site of a haunting, on occasion people will go there and expect to see the ghost. If they don't, disappointment surely follows. So the next best thing is invention. They think back and imagine that they saw something.

A ley line runs through this area, which possibly assists the apparition to appear. There is a lot of evidence to suggest that ghosts are more likely to be seen on or near to ley lines. As far as I am aware, the only other country that has such a rich tradition of roadside apparitions is South Africa.

I can remember reading some years ago of the work of a vicar who strongly believed accident blackspots to be caused by the ghosts of victims of previous accidents. He claimed to have some success when he performed an exorcism at these sites, cleansing the road of negativity. We all know of such accident blackspots. Indeed, when I was growing up, there was one just outside my own village of Harpole. I lost count of the number of accidents and deaths here as I was growing up.

I can remember reading about an Anglican clergyman who regularly exorcized places on the road where a high incidence of accidents occurred. It was his belief that some spots became loaded with negative energy and unrested souls. He reported a lessening of such incidents after these services were performed.

SOME CONCLUSIONS

THIS BOOK is the culmination of over two years of research, interviewing witnesses and visiting sites in the faint hope of gathering some evidence, with tape-recorder and camera at the ready. However, as any hunter knows, your quarry is least likely to appear when you are armed and ready for him.

This research has inevitably led me to some new conclusions. As our brains are much more than just a cluster of cells, nerves and fibres, thoughts can escape the bony confines of the skull and affect people and things around us. Discoveries in the realm of quantum physics bear this out, and physicists now believe that the observer in an experiment can affect that experiment at a molecular level – so the course of an atom can be changed by the expectations of the scientist taking part. Therefore, if we suppose that the mind can escape the restrictions of the body, even in only a small (yet measurable) way, then surely the death of that body might be no barrier to the continued activity of that mind? Possibly, it can go on thinking, feeling – and affecting matter.

I also believe that some hauntings, especially those of a negative kind, can be due in part to environmental triggers. As we know, the earth is one vast magnet and has in its crust many cracks and fissures, which at times of stress on its plates release various gases. These could affect both people and animals. In addition, the presence of hidden underground streams could exert an influence on electrical fields. All these naturally occurring electrical, magnetic and hydrodynamic forces could well play some part in the puzzle. Indeed, I recently read of research by doctors in Spain into how magnetic fields play a part in human mood. They have taken to alleviating depression in some patients using magnets that are attached to the patient's head for short periods each day, and the results are already promising. Often, a side-effect noticed by those at haunted locations is a palpable feeling of depression, and I'm sure there is a link here.

Mediumship is a different matter and still remains largely unproven. This ability is akin to a design fault in the powerhouse of the brain. Individuals lacking this ability seem to have the curtains up at a window in the mind, shutting out this parallel dimension that seems to infringe upon our own – perhaps mediums are missing the curtains altogether?

I feel that we are very close to solving parts of the mystery behind recorded ghostly activity. If we can find the trigger – be it atmospheric conditions, vibration, manipulation of objects or whatever – theoretically we could then listen in to and observe snippets of our past. Dialects long forgotten would be discovered, while buildings and other relics could yield valuable information that had hitherto been locked into them.

Albert Budden's work on the Hutchison effect also provides some answers. I have seen video footage of Hutchison's so-called 'poltergeist machine' at work, the effects mimicking in part what can happen during a poltergeist outbreak.

As time goes by and, hopefully, we shed more light on these phenomena, some of the fear that people often feel when seeing a ghost – a fear which is seldom justified – will disappear. As I continue with this research, I feel ever more sure of the inherent reality (albeit one that is difficult to quantify) behind many of these ghostly experiences – and the search continues.

BIBLIOGRAPHY

The following publications have either been referred to in the text or will be of interest to ghost-hunters or anyone interested in the subject.

Budden, Albert, *Allergies and Aliens*. Redwood Books

Eason, Cassandra, *Ghost Encounters*. Blandford, 1998.

Gordon, Stuart, *The Paranormal: An Illustrated Encyclopedia*. Headline Books, 1992.

Hapgood, Sarah, *The World's Greatest Ghost and Poltergeist Stories*. Foulsham, 1994.

Harrison, Thomas, *Fire From Heaven*. Pan Books, 1977.

Keneally, Thomas, *Schindler's Ark*. Sphere, 1986.

Lyon-Playfair, Guy, *This House is Haunted*. Souvenir Press, 1980.

Osborne-Thomason, Natalie, *Walking Through Walls*. Janus Publishing, 1997.

Wood, Robert, *The Widow of Borley*. Gerald Duckworth, 1992.

The *Fortean Times* magazine is published monthly by John Brown Publishing.

INDEX